You Have to Go
to School... YOU'RE
THE
TEACHER!

THIRD EDITION

**300+ CLASSROOM
MANAGEMENT
STRATEGIES
TO MAKE YOUR
JOB EASIER
AND MORE FUN**

Renee Rosenblum-Lowden With Felicia Lowden Kimmel

CORWIN PRESS
A SAGE Company
Thousand Oaks, CA 91320

For information:

Corwin Press
A SAGE Company
2455 Teller Road
Thousand Oaks, California 91320
www.corwinpress.com

SAGE Ltd.
1 Oliver's Yard
55 City Road
London EC1Y 1SP
United Kingdom

SAGE India Pvt. Ltd.
B 1/I 1 Mohan Cooperative
     Industrial Area
Mathura Road, New Delhi 110 044
India

SAGE Asia-Pacific Pte. Ltd.
33 Pekin Street #02–01
Far East Square
Singapore 048763

Printed in the United States of America

Library of Congress Cataloging-in-Publication Data

Rosenblum-Lowden, Renee.
You have to go to school . . . you're the teacher! :300+ classroom management strategies to make your job easier and more fun / Renee Rosenblum-Lowden and Felicia Lowden Kimmel. – 3rd ed.
        p. cm.
Includes bibliographical references and index.
ISBN 978-1-4129-5121-0 (cloth)
ISBN 978-1-4129-5122-7 (pbk.)
    1. Teachers—United States. 2. Teaching—United States.
3. First-year teachers—United States. 4. Classroom management—United States.
I. Kimmel, Felicia Lowden. II. Title.

LB1775.2.R67 2008
371.102—dc22   2007029944

This book is printed on acid-free paper.

07   08   09   10   10   9   8   7   6   5   4   3   2   1

Acquisitions Editor:	Jessica Allan
Editorial Assistant:	Joanna Coelho
Production Editor:	Libby Larson
Copy Editor:	Renee Willers
Typesetter:	C&M Digitals (P) Ltd.
Proofreader:	Theresa Kay
Indexer:	Will Ragsdale
Cover Designer:	Lisa Riley

Praise for Renee Rosenblum-Lowden and
the Second Edition of *You Have to Go to School—You're the Teacher!*

"Ms. Rosenblum-Lowden writ[...] humor and wonderful insights. The book will be a staple for every new [...] perience."

—[...]*da Lavinsky, Guidance Counselor, NYC*

"I read the evaluations on Frid[...] ber of teachers who indicated their joy in hearing your presentation by providing a rating of 10, when 3 was the highest score. Many teachers liked your speaking at the closing of the orientation. I look forward to seeing you again next year."

—*Aggie Langan, Coordinator for Staff Development, Cecil County Public Schools, MD*

"Your energy alone lit up the room, and in conjunction with your inspiring words, experienced advice, and genuine care, our students could not have been more moved. You are gifted with the way in which you share your knowledge, and it is no wonder you are a sought-after presenter. You are a beacon for so many."

—*Lisa Twiss, Instructor, Johns Hopkins University, Baltimore, MD*

"Renee Rosenblum-Lowden reminds us that classroom management is both an art and a skill, as she shares her mastery of both in this slender volume filled with practical instruction, charm, and wit. When I observed her in the classroom, I thought her magic was intuitive and undefinable, but she has made her techniques accessible to every good teacher."

—*Pearl Newman Sloane, Former Principal, Eugenio Maria De Hostos Middle School, Brooklyn, NY*

"Ms. Lowden's presentation was practical, witty, relative, and timely. All the teachers received a copy of her book *You Have to Go to School—You're the Teacher*, and on their evaluation forms more than one hundred teachers had only positive comments. It is obvious Ms. Lowden's presentation was overwhelmingly received."

—*Jean Wadley, Facilitator, Stafford County Public Schools, VA*

"I want to commend you on your presentation of your book, *You Have to Go to School—You're the Teacher*. Your sense of humor and presentation style are engaging and stimulating. I was impressed with the energy level you brought to the room."

—*Jephta Nguherimo, MSTA/Uniserv Director, Prince George's Education Association, MD*

"Thank you for speaking to our faculty on classroom management. You have a special talent for making people feel at ease. Our teachers are looking forward to trying some of the strategies you shared with us from your book, *You Have to Go to School—You're the Teacher*. I know the students will appreciate them."

—*Madelyn Ball, Assistant Principal for Staff Development, Our Lady of Good Counsel High School, MD*

"Great job and lots of wonderful feedback. My staff told me how much they learned from your presentation. You definitely made the subject interesting for the participants and we look forward to reading your book."

—*Vivianne Waldron, Coordinator of Staff Development, Highlands Country School Board, FL*

"All who attended the End of the Year Celebration made a special effort to let me know how much they enjoyed both interacting with you and listening to your presentation. I am certain they will be referring to your book, *You Have to Go to School—You're the Teacher* for their entire careers."

—*Andrea Mucci, Manager for New Teacher Support, Anne Arundel County, MD*

"Thank you for your wonderful presentation to the teachers in Polk County. You did such an awesome job presenting such vital information in an easy to understand, practical manner."

— *Kathy Giroux, Principal, Wendell Watson Elementary School, Lakeland, FL*

"You were, as always, wonderful! I haven't seen the feedback forms yet. However, I asked several of the newbies how the small group sessions went and they could do nothing but rave about how much they enjoyed interacting with you in a small group."

—Denise Fry, Mentor Resource Teacher, Washington County Public Schools, Hagerstown, MD

"Your strategies for the classroom were well received by everyone who attended. The energy and enthusiasm you brought to your programs captivated the audience with your humorous and practical advice that we can pass along to prospective and beginning teachers as they work to survive in the classroom."

—Christina E. MacGill, Associate Director Career Services, The Pennsylvania State University, Forging New Alliances in Education, MAASCUS Conference

"Each year, Renee Rosenblum-Lowden shares her book and her experiences with our teachers. She motivates them and provides them with a real look into building classroom communities. Our new teachers have valued this experience, sharing such comments as:"

"My excitement for teaching was refreshed! She gave many strategies that could be used in the classroom, such as building classroom community."

"I have read Renee's book twice now to get more ideas."

"Renee is great to listen to and the book is wonderful."

"I thought Ms. Lowden was an awesome presenter. Her enthusiasm and anecdotal stories captured my interest the entire time!"

"WOW . . . I really enjoyed this seminar. Ms. Lowden was a great speaker that opened my eyes to what TO do and what NOT to do and how to do both effectively to manage my classroom."

"This session gave me many different REAL ideas and strategies to classroom management, which I found useful in my classroom."

"Books like hers are what new teachers need!"

"What an inspiring guest speaker!"

"Absolutely loved it! What was needed right before the holiday break. She really connected with the audience and had some great strategies and answers for teachers."

"I sat down over the weekend and read the whole thing in one sitting."

— Jeff Maher, Director of Professional and Organizational Development, St. Mary's County Public Schools, Leonardtown, MD

"All teachers, new or experienced, will find something helpful in this book."

—Review in **Apple**—*Professional staff magazine for Fairfax, VA Public Schools*

"Your presentation was uplifting and an overwhelming success. Your presentation based on your book, *You Have to Go to School—You're the Teacher* generated many accolades and was so well received by all our participants."

—Michael Banks, Principal, Louverture School, East Orange, NJ

"I couldn't imagine a teacher anywhere who would not benefit from this wonderful book! In a personal and informal tone, Renee shares clever strategies for handling everyday classroom situations. Her insight provides a 'guide' for all teachers, novice or experienced, to help them manage every aspect of the classroom, from homework policies and lost pencils, to overuse of the health room and 'dressing for success' in the classroom. The scenarios are honest and many times humorous, and her techniques are practical and effective. I highly recommend this book . . . I absolutely love it! It's an easy-to-use, quick reference book filled with information that I presently use and will continue to use daily in my teaching."

—Denise Harris, Nursery School Teacher, B'nai Shalom of Olney Nursery School, Montgomery County Public Schools

"I met someone who helped turn my life around, a very special teacher named Ms. Lowden."

— Jay-Z, Teen People

Contents

Preface   xv
   Acknowledgments   xvi

About the Authors   xix

Introduction   xxi

Part I: Tips for New and Student Teachers   1

1. Odds and Ends for Beginners   3
   Put Loved Ones on Notice   3
   Your Students Didn't Sleep Last Night Either!   3
   The Mentor Teacher   4
   Dress Like a Grown-Up   4
   Students Do Get Crushes   5
   Overplan   5
   Flexible Personal Expectations   6
   Everyone Else's Plans Are Better   6
   The Clerical Work Blues   7
   Ask Teachers for Help   7
   Observing Other Teachers   7
   Teacher Negativity   8
   Just Say No   8

Part II: Beginning a Winning Year   9

2. They're Not Here Yet   11
   Get to School Early   11
   Organizing the Room   11
   Put Up Diplomas   12
   Say Cheese   12

Don't Be Caught Unprepared or Late 12
Enthusiasm Is Caught, Not Taught 13
Friendly, But Not Buddies 13
Personal Records Debate 14

3. They're Here **15**
The Rush to Seats 15
Seating Ideas 15
Don't Seat by Height—Or Gender 16
Dealing for Groups 17
Record Keeping Questionnaire 17
Now and Later Cards 18
The First Day "Sneaker" 18
Fun Introductions 19
Put Your Name—and Phone Number?—on the Board 19
You've Got Mail 20
Tangible Class Guidelines and Rules 21
Let Students Set Rules and Consequences 21
You Own the Limelight 21
You Can Always Ease Up 22
Sit With Your Students 22
Greet Students at the Door 23
Document! Document! Document! 23
Yowks! Five Minutes Left 24
End the First Day on an Up Note 24

4. They're Gone and You Survived! **25**
Everything Can Be Redone 25
You're Not a Shrink 25
Don't Take Their Behavior Personally 26
You Can't Win 'Em All 26
Go Home and Chill Out 26

Part III: Helping Students Be Responsible **29**

5. Establishing Routines **31**
Creatures of Habit 31
The Standardized Notebook 31
The "Do Now" or "Warm Up" 32
The Aim of "Aim" 32
Class Wrap-Ups 32
When to Give Out Worksheets 33

You Teach, Not Videos   33
Who Dismisses?   34

6. Have Them Come (and Stay) Prepared   **35**
You Are Not the Supply Store   35
"You Owe Me a Favor"   35
Bless the Bargain Stores   36
Collateral, Please   36
Strings Attached   37
Creative Pencils   37
The Sharpener Cover   37
Pencils = Charity   38
Swapping   38
Scrap Paper   38

7. Homework Strategies   **41**
The Importance of Homework   41
The Homework Spot   41
Numbering Homework   42
Collecting Homework   42
Hand In a Blank Sheet   42
Sign on the Dotted Line   43
Homework Buddies   43
H-O-M-E-W-O-R-K   43
Oops Pass   44
Homework Penalty (With Room for Redemption)   44
Homework Helper . . . You!   45

8. Bathroom Breaks   **47**
The Sign-Out Book   47
"Can You Wait a Minute?"   47
The Visual Pass   48
Secret Code   48
Bathroom Coupons   48
Respecting the Restroom   49
That Time of the Month   49

9. Empowering Students   **51**
We Make Our Own Choices   51
The Right to Pass   51
The Sanctuary   52
Tacit Approval   52

One Is a Rat—Ten Is Power   53
The "Many Kids Told Me" Fib   54
Don't Call Home   54
Softening the Call Home   55
Tons of Quizzes   55
Offer Choices   56
Confer for Grades   56
"Class"—The Collective Noun   57
Independent Reading, With Twinkies!   57
Go With the Roll   58
Incorporating Fads   58
Did They Learn What You Taught?   58
Role Reversal or Role-Playing   59
"Am I Boring?"   59
Classroom Suggestion Box   60
A Fun Way to Limit Slang   60
Don't Overcorrect   61
Student Revenge: Your Personal Evaluation   61
"Help . . . I'm Being Observed!"   62
I Bragged About You   62

10. Setting Consequences   **63**
Every Act Has a Consequence   63
Coupons, Tickets, Marbles, or "Money"   63
Sweets or No Sweets   64
Start With a 99%   64
Conduct Sheets   65
Torture Sheets   65
When to Call Home   66
Avoiding Confrontation   66

11. Preventing Showdowns   **67**
Going on Automatic   67
Everything Is Embarrassing   67
Humor, Not Sarcasm   68
The Biggest No-No: "Only Kidding"   68
"Shut Up!—Not!"   69
"I Told You So"   69
Avoid Arguments   69
Globalizing   69

Choose Your Battles 70
Start All Over 70
Beware of Empty Threats 71
No Spur-of-the-Moment Rules 71
Set Up Winning Situations 71
Plagiarism 72
Don't Force Students to Lie 72
Make Rules Specific: Narrow Them Down 72
No Sides 73
Time-Out 73
No Comparisons 73
Never Attack Personally 74
Distractions 74

12. Alternatives to Yelling **75**
The "Teacher" Look 75
The "Excuse Me" Smile 75
The Lowered Voice 76
The Art of Gestures 76
Clap, Clap 76
Hurry, Shut Off the Lights! 77
Praising One 77
Initials on Board 77
Visual Commands 78
"I Am Waiting" 78
The Bellhop Bell 78
Stop Teaching 79
The Tardy Quiz 79
Early Bird Special 79
An Imaginary Friend 80
Word of the Day 80
R-E-C-E-S-S 80

13. Knowing Your Audience **81**
Group Dynamics 81
Division of Labor 81
Don't Play "I Gotcha" 82
Deceiving Looks 82
Kids Have Bad Days, Too 83
Negative Attention Seekers 83

Good Kids Can Do Bad Things 83
Hold Students to Different Standards 84
If You Don't Try, You Can't Fail 84
Too Much Push on Sports 85
"Can We Really Be Anything We Want?" 85
Audio or Visual? 85
Check the Senses 86
Respect Privacy 86
A Secret Is a Secret, Unless . . . 87
Ignore Reputation 87
Permissive Versus Overly Permissive 88
Cultural Differences 88
What Language Is Spoken at Home? 89
Quality, Not Quantity 89
Confusing Neatness With Responsibility 89
Describe a Fight to a Potential Pugilist 90
The Sound-Off Minute 90

Part IV: Showing You're on the Same Team **91**

14. Communicating Like a Pro **93**
Acknowledge Feelings 93
Never Deny Perception 93
Use "I" Messages 94
"Let's" Instead of "You" 94
Interchange Gender Pronouns 94
Limit the "You Shoulds" 95
One-on-One 95
How to Listen 96
Make Limits Total Rather Than Partial 96
State Rules Impersonally 97
Vague Allegations 97
Describe What You See (or Don't See) 97
Pick a Rule and Stick to It 98
Stay Simple: One Word or Sentence Will Do 98
The Desk Drummer 99
Would You Talk to an Adult That Way? 99
Don't Futurize 99
Paraphrase 100
Don't Mix Criticism With Praise 100

Cursing—Yes or No? 100
Forced Apologies Not Accepted 101
The Double Message 101
What Would Another Teacher Tell Me? 102

15. Being Fair **103**
Admit When You Are Wrong 103
Admit When You Don't Know Something 103
Never Break a Promise 104
Never Demand a Promise 104
"I'm in a Bad Mood" 105
"This Hurts Me More Than It Hurts You" 105
No "Boys Will Be Boys" 106
Etiquette Pitfalls 106
Please and Thank You 106
Gauge the Amount of Homework 107

16. Bonding Strategies **109**
"I'm on Your Side" 109
Being Vulnerable: Share a Giggle 109
Relating Your Own Experiences 110
Staying Neutral 110
Those Special Few Minutes 111
15 Seconds of Fame 111
Creative Excuses 112
Bend the Rules 112
Journals 112
Know When You Are Overly Involved 113
Read Aloud to Your Students 113
Giant Calendar 114
Celebrate Birthdays 114
Catch the Spirit 114
"I Thought of You" 115
Morning Meetings 115
Class Solutions 116
Lowden's Life Lessons (Or, Teaching Winning Ways) 116
Decorating Your Room . . . Again 117
Assure Students You Will Tell Their Parents
   Something Wonderful 117
Thank Them for the Joy They Bring 117

Part V: Building Confidence Through Earned Praise   **119**

17. Self-Esteem Strategies   **121**

Praise, Praise, Praise—But Don't Overpraise   121
Acknowledge Improvements   122
Overgrading   122
Confidence Grading   122
Enthusiastic Credit When Credit Is Due   123
Put-Ups, Not Put-Downs   123
Respect Uniqueness   123
Leaders Need to Follow   124
Don't Rush to Correct   124
Call Home for the "Average" Student   124
"I Knew You Could Do It" (and More)   125
A Little White Lie   125
"You're a Late Bloomer"   126
Tracking   126
Some of Us Can't Spell   127
Wonderful Comments on Paper   127
Post Each Student's Work   128
"I Got a 97%! What Did You Get?"   128

Part VI: Safety   **129**

18. Personal, Physical, and Professional Safety   **131**

To Touch or Not to Touch   131
Face the Door   131
Never Release a Student to a Stranger   132
Never Throw a Student Out of Your Room   132
Don't Break Up Fights   132
Screen the Videos   133
Your School's Emergency Plan   133
The Cafeteria   134
Keep the Door Open   134
Never Leave Classes Unattended   134
You Are Neither a Pharmacist nor a Doctor   135
Do Not Drive Your Students in Your Car   135
Report Every Accident   136
Trust Your Gut Feelings and Follow Instincts   136
Go Home Already!   137

Part VII: Using Your Support System   **139**

19. Working With Parents   **141**
    Meet Parents Right Away   141
    Send Home an Introduction   141
    Accommodate Parents   142
    Inform Parents Early On   142
    Tear on the Dotted Line   143
    Parents and the Internet   143
    Getting Parents Involved   143
    Special Relative Day   144
    Call *Both* Parents   144
    Students at Parent Conferences?   144
    Teacher as Middleman   145
    Parent-Teacher Conference Management   146
    Assuring Parents   146
    The Defensive Parent   147
    Parents and Homework   147
    Children as Dream Fulfillers   148
    Parents *Knowing* More Than You   148
    The Blame Game   149
    Don't Stereotype   149
    Beware of the Answering Machine   150
    *67   150

20. Working With the School Support Team   **151**
    Partner With the Counselors   151
    Cover Your Back . . . When to Consult Your
        School Counselor or Psychologist   151
    Conflict Resolution   152
    Cooperative Teacher Input   152
    Buddy Teacher   152
    Other Teachers' Successes   153
    Confronting Other Teachers   153
    No Gossiping About Your Students   154
    Teacher Competition   154
    Do You Float?   155
    Field Trip Protocol   155
    Helping Substitute Teachers   156
    Preparing Your Students for Your Absence   157

Evaluating Substitute Teachers   157
Partnerships With Local Shops, Libraries,
    and Bookstores   158
Getting Along With the "Boss"   158
The Teachers' Union   159
Keep Those Skills Sharp   159
The Really Important People   160

Part VIII: Parting Shots   **161**

21. See You Next Year!   **163**
Is Teaching What You Really Want to Do?   163
Keep in Touch   163
The Portfolio   163
Holiday "Blahs"   164
Burnout Prevention   164
Only a Few More Months 'til Summer Vacation   165

Suggested Readings   **167**
Index   **169**

Preface

Since I have addressed thousands of teachers, I have learned two things . . . one is we hate having PowerPoints read to us, and two is we rarely have time to read prefaces to books, so I will try to make this short.

As a result of the success of the book, I have been invited to keynote throughout the country sharing my enthusiasm and passion for a career that I have loved for more than 25 years. I enjoy the opportunity to make teachers laugh while at the same time providing them with teacher-tested classroom management strategies. I think it is important to make sure my readers understand that there might be some strategies you disagree with, but hopefully there will be many new ones that will help in managing your classrooms. We all have different teaching styles, and what works for one, may not work for another.

Whether we are veterans, new teachers, or student teachers, we all need new and exciting ideas. Many school districts have bought the book for their new teachers, and many schools have bought the book for their entire staff, while many colleges use the book for student teaching seminars. Many school districts have book groups and have used my book for discussion. It is thrilling for me to be able to share ideas with so many.

What is most exciting about this new edition is that I am collaborating with my daughter, Felicia Lowden Kimmel, who is contributing insights from another perspective—that of the guidance counselor. She had been a classroom teacher for many years before becoming a counselor; as a result, she views teaching from many vantage points, and her input is invaluable.

So enjoy the book, and feel free to e-mail me at prejteach2@ aol.com if you need any help with classroom management; but most of all, enjoy the greatest profession there is.

ACKNOWLEDGMENTS

I would like to thank the following people:

- Pearl Newman Sloane, my first principal, who remains one of my dearest and most respected friends. She taught me one of the best lessons of my career. After my first year of teaching, she offered me a special program, telling me I was one of the best teachers she had ever seen. I looked at her modestly and said, "I'm not really that good." She asked me if I would go to a doctor who said he wasn't really that good. She added, "You're good. Don't deny it." So to show I learned that lesson, I will tell you right now, "This book is really good!"

- The staff of Enrich—The School for Social Action, for proving that a good team can do anything. We came as close to a perfect educational experience as I have ever experienced. Thanks to Michelle Fratti for giving us the freedom to create an incredible school and to Sarah Mercer for her input.

- The dynamic women of FSN for their support and wisdom.

- My husband, Michael, for listening to all my school stories, for offering great suggestions, and for all his incredible insights.

- My father, who told me a cute joke many years ago—which is now the title of this book—and my mother, who told anyone who would listen what a good teacher I was. I wish they were here today.

- Rap artist Jay-Z (known to me as Shawn Carter), who was my student 25 years ago, for giving me my 15 minutes of fame by giving me credit publicly for having a positive impact on his life. He is proof to me and to teachers everywhere that we can make an impression on students without even realizing it.

- All my students who have brought me so much happiness and who have enriched my life so much over the past 25 years. I hope they are living healthy and productive lives.

Corwin Press wishes to thank the following peer reviewers for their editorial insight and guidance:

Yolanda Abel, Instructor
Johns Hopkins University, School of Education
Baltimore, MD

Jacie Bejster, Principal
Crafton Elementary School, Pittsburgh, PA

April Keck DeGennaro, Gifted Teacher
Fayette County Board of Education
Fayetteville, GA

Loukea N. Kovanis-Wilson, Chemistry Instructor
Clarkston High School, Clarkston, MI

Elaine Mayer, Lead New Teacher Coach
New Teacher Support and Development
Oakland Unified School District, Oakland, CA

Renee Peoples, NBPTS, Fourth Grade Teacher
West Elementary, Bryson City, NC

Donnan Stoicovy, Elementary Principal
Park Forest Elementary School
State College, PA

Cynthia Wilson, Associate Professor
University of Illinois at Springfield
Springfield, IL

Mother: Get up, it's time to go to school.
Son: I don't want to go.
Mother: But you have to go to school!
Son: I'm afraid the kids won't like me, and I don't want to go!
Mother: You have to go to school!
Son: I'm too nervous.
Mother: You *have* to go to school . . . You're the *teacher!*

About the Authors

Renee Rosenblum-Lowden has taught children and adolescents for more than 25 years in the New York City school system. Currently, she is sharing her love for teaching by presenting seminars and keynote speeches to new and veteran teachers throughout the country, as well as to student teachers at various universities. She uses a sense of humor while arming them with great strategies for making classrooms safe and fun—while always being in control. She has developed a curriculum called Prejudice Awareness, using consciousness-raising techniques and incorporating her training in conflict resolution. She was selected by the NYC Board of Education to train teachers in this subject.

Ms. Rosenblum-Lowden has conducted workshops for improving communication with children and adolescents, using nonconfrontational strategies for parents and teachers. Having taught family living and sex education classes, she has unique insights into the needs of her students. Ms. Rosenblum-Lowden did her undergraduate work at Long Island University and studied at The New School for Social Research and New York University. She continues to be a social activist. She is a transplanted New Yorker who is now living in Columbia, Maryland, with her husband, Michael, and their dog, Susie B. Anthony.

Felicia Lowden Kimmel grew up in Brooklyn, New York. She began her career in education as a high school English to Speakers of Other Languages (ESOL) and English teacher in San Francisco before returning east to teach in the Washington, D.C. area. She was selected to lead a Peer Mediation program at Annandale High School in Fairfax County, Virginia. Her program received a great deal of attention and received national praise after the tragedy at Columbine. She was spotlighted as a panelist for NPR's "All Things Considered" and was a featured guest on WPGC's "Stop the Violence." After several years in this capacity, she joined the high school's guidance department while still continuing her involvement in conflict resolution. Ms. Lowden Kimmel has also worked with school districts' faculties on understanding prejudice.

Currently, Ms. Lowden Kimmel is working as a school counselor in Montgomery County, Maryland. She lives in Olney with her husband, Troy, their two daughters, Isabella and Lexi, and their dog, Maggie.

Introduction

A funny thing happened on my way to giving a seminar on a curriculum I developed called Prejudice Awareness. . . .

When my daughter Felicia was a new teacher taking classes at San Francisco State University, she talked about my course with her fellow students. Her classmates kept saying that they would love to hear more about it, which led her professor to invite me to address the group. I gladly leapt at the opportunity, as it was a wonderful excuse to see my daughter. (I didn't need an "excuse" to see her, but I did have to justify the 3,000-mile plane trip!)

Well, I planned everything I was going to say but lived in perpetual fear that I would stand up there and re-create some of those awkward moments from what seemed a lifetime ago—when my daughter was a cringing preteen and teenager being humiliated by everything I said and everything I did. I had to keep reminding myself that it was her idea to invite me.

When the big night came and I was about to speak, I realized I had left my note cards in the computer room, which was now locked. While Felicia was getting the security guards to open the door to retrieve my notes (and hence, rescue me), I was sure that her memories of being embarrassed by me were alive and well in her mind. While she was gone, I noticed all the anxieties that those in her class were sharing among themselves about their own students, the other teachers, their lack of control, and their insecurities in general. I remembered those days and those anxieties.

When I finally began speaking, I looked at them and said, "When I was a new teacher, I asked myself what I would want in a teacher if I were one of the students. I knew I would want someone to teach me in an environment that was fun, yet demanding. I hope I did that.

"Now, tonight, I look at you—new teachers—and I ask myself yet again, what would I want if I were sitting where you are? I would want a real live classroom teacher—a person who has 175 children passing through her classroom every day and has all kinds of strategies to cope with the daily routines and crises that occur—to tell me her 'tricks of the trade.'"

Their heads were nodding so furiously, I knew I was right on target. For the next two hours, I shared with them the skills I had accumulated from my contact with so many thousands of young people between 8 and 17 years of age, and from the wisdom I had amassed by having students share their journals and personal thoughts with me. I had also led parent-teacher workshops for many years and was trained in the specialty area of conflict resolution, and I was able to draw on those experiences. After sharing teaching strategies for two hours, I discussed my course on prejudice for another two hours. And guess what? My daughter winked and gave me two thumbs up. Puberty was over . . . I hadn't humiliated her and she is a contributor to this new edition. Who would have thought?

Since that day I have shared my strategies and ideas in workshops with countless other teachers who provided valuable feedback and encouragement. This book has evolved out of that process.

My goal in writing this book is to give teachers the book I wish I'd had when I was first struggling in the classroom—a "teacher-friendly" book to tell me what to expect, how to make my classroom a place that students can't wait to get to and where they want to learn; a common-sense book with a sense of humor, written by someone who has been in the classroom—and who loved every day of it. I also hope to help veteran teachers prevent "burnout" by offering fresh ideas and sharing stories with which they can identify.

In this book there are over 300 strategies to help preservice, new, and experienced teachers develop rapport with students and manage everyday school problems. Major topics include how to start a successful year, how to help students learn responsibility, how to communicate with honesty and fairness, how to build students' confidence, how to prevent confrontation and showdowns, and how to work effectively with parents and school staff.

Let me express my gratitude to all the teachers who have been kind enough to share how the first two editions of this book have helped them in their classrooms. What has delighted me is the diversity of readers, from the student teacher to the seasoned veteran.

To all teachers who are looking for new strategies, I hope I provide those for you. I am sure there are some strategies to which you will take exception, but I hope there are many more that you will try and find effective. To all new teachers, I congratulate you on choosing a wonderfully fulfilling career, and I hope my experiences and strategies will help you. Remember, a few of these might work for you, and you will probably invent some for yourself that may be even more successful. Good luck—and make a difference!

I invite you to e-mail me with comments or queries:

Prejteach2@aol.com

Renee Rosenblum-Lowden

We dedicate this book to
Michael and Troy—the loves of our lives
Isabella Paige and Alexis Lily—the joys of our lives
Irving and Peggy Rosenblum—in memory

PART I

Tips for New and Student Teachers

I t has often been said that the most creative ideas come from the beginners, not from the experts.

People who have been teaching a long time are often called "experts"; some are and some are not. There are some teachers who have to duck paper airplanes (on a good day) who are considered experts merely because they have been teaching forever. Not necessarily so! Most of you are recently out of school and heavily armed with this wonderful strength I call "unjaded idealism." New teachers, fresh out of teaching programs, have shared all kinds of wonderful strategies and philosophies.

Don't be afraid to experiment, and don't be afraid to use all that creativity you know you have. It takes a very short time for a truly talented teacher to become an "expert."

AUTHOR'S NOTE: To make the book gender inclusive, I have interchanged pronouns throughout, and I hope you will do the same in your classrooms.

CHAPTER ONE

Odds and Ends for Beginners

PUT LOVED ONES ON NOTICE

The first few weeks of teaching are probably going to be filled with stress. Plead with your friends and family to bear with you. You may be short with them, and you may perhaps even use them to vent what you didn't vent in the classroom. Warn them that you will probably fall asleep the second you get home and perhaps sleep through a good part of the weekend.

There will be days when you will have loads of "adorable" stories about "adorable" students. I will warn you of something your loved ones may be too kind to tell you. You may be *boring* them. It's like someone telling you about a neighbor running off with someone else. Unless you know the neighbor, who cares? If you notice their eyes rolling, it may be time to change the subject. But don't worry; there really are many people who will love to hear your stories. (Other teachers who know your students serve as fine audiences.)

YOUR STUDENTS DIDN'T SLEEP LAST NIGHT EITHER!

You may have not slept a wink before your first day, but neither did many of your colleagues and most of your students. No matter how many years we have been teaching, the first day of school always arouses some anxiety and always feels like the first year all over again. There is a good chance you will toss and turn and then be panicked that you will fall asleep right at your desk. Relax! When the adrenaline kicks in, you will be just fine. The reality is that your students are so focused on themselves that they won't notice your anxieties.

THE MENTOR TEACHER

Student teachers always ask me how I suggest they tell their mentoring teacher that what he or she is doing is wrong. *Well, don't even think about it!* You are a guest in your mentor's classroom and should behave that way. We have to look at our mentor teachers as we would our parents. You know we are stuck with them unless they are absolutely awful, and only then can we usually do something about it. However, a good idea might be to offer "suggestions" or to ask if you may try something a little different. A good mentor teacher usually asks for your input, at which time you may feel free to express yourself. You are there to learn from, not to teach, your mentor even though we both know you have so much to share.

One of my student teachers had a wonderful outlook. She had taught under a rigid autocrat who terrorized his students and even scared her. She said, "I learned from him what not to do!"

DRESS LIKE A GROWN-UP

Oh, I can't believe I'm saying this! When I began teaching, I prided myself on being a nonconformist and insisted on wearing jeans to school. But this was a problem because I was young when I began teaching and I looked close in age to my students. And guess what? They treated me as if I were one of them.

It may sound nice, but as the authority in the classroom, you have to distance yourself a bit. One way to do so is to dress the part. Dressing like a professional gives you a head start in your classroom. It says, "I am the teacher and you are the student." Studies have shown that discipline techniques work better when a teacher looks more professional. I didn't believe them until the day I had to get dressed up to go somewhere after school and found an indefinable difference in how my students reacted to me. It was definitely positive.

A friend of mine who teaches junior high school students was told by one of his students, "You must really like us. You come to school all dressed up, as though you are going someplace special."

Eventually you can dress however you feel is appropriate, but in the beginning I suggest you dress like the professional you are. Also, keep in mind that some adolescent students develop "crushes" on their teachers, so I'm even going to go so far as to tell you to err on the conservative side.

STUDENTS DO GET CRUSHES

It happens! No matter how young the student, you may become the object of his or her adoration. Please be sensitive to this, as these fragile little hearts are easily broken by a patronizing laugh. Be careful to keep a distance because students often become very possessive and even get upset at the thought of you having a social life.

I had a student (who came up to my waist) who told me his dream of beating up my husband. When I asked him why, he said he just didn't like him. (By the way, he'd never met him!)

With older students, especially high schoolers, teachers have to be especially conscious about not sending out signals or responding to those being sent.

OVERPLAN

As a new teacher, it is impossible to gauge how long your first day's lesson plans will last. You should have your introductions, course expectations, classroom and school rules, temporary seating arrangements, and some homework assignments prepared. It's a good idea to have additional lessons "just in case." I have had years when I never even got up to the rules and other years when I seemed to be done in a minute and a half. The dynamics of a group vary so much that it is impossible to plan a 45-minute lesson and expect each group to react the same way. Remember, it is hard to "wing it," especially with a brand-new group. There are always perceptive students who know you are not prepared and can make you look as if you are not in control.

Have two hours of lessons for your one-hour class. It's a great habit to get into. Remember, if you aren't prepared, how can you expect your students to be? My money is on you, though, because a new teacher usually overplans in the beginning.

FLEXIBLE PERSONAL EXPECTATIONS

Please go easy on yourself if your students are not reading and writing at the level you think they should be. Too often teachers set goals for their students that are unrealistic. Before you are convinced you are not teaching your students anything and are about to quit to work in a bakery, find out what limitations your students might have. Read their records, speak to their other teachers, and discuss their progress, or lack of progress, with their parents. Some children may improve slightly while others learn in leaps and bounds. You cannot expect all your students to learn at the same pace, and sometimes you have to be content knowing that a slight improvement is what they are capable of at this time. If a student is not showing progress and you believe she should be doing better, you should speak to the guidance counselor or the resource teacher to see what can be done to help your student . . . and that doesn't include devaluing yourself and your teaching ability.

EVERYONE ELSE'S PLANS ARE BETTER

While we are talking about plans, I hear so many new teachers tell me they are sure everyone else has better lesson plans. They always feel theirs are not good enough. Don't fret. Those you admire are probably wondering what great ideas you've got up your sleeve. Your plans are probably fine, but self-doubt can be a great motivator. Whenever I hear people complain about inexperienced teachers, I chuckle to myself. You see, I love working with new teachers because I usually think their plans are better than mine!

THE CLERICAL WORK BLUES

Many of us are "organizationally challenged." I have seen teachers allow paperwork to overwhelm them, and I hope you do not allow that to happen to you. Do not procrastinate. Get those reports in on time. You do not want your principal or department head hounding you (especially when we demand that our students have their work in on time). If you do not get your attendance reports in on time, it holds up the school secretary. If you do not get the report card grades entered, it holds up your colleagues. If you do not get your lesson plans in on time, you may get a letter in your file that will not please you. Get yourself into a routine and know when things are due and do not leave them for the last minute. (Okay, we may not be able to do that all the time, but we have got to try!)

ASK TEACHERS FOR HELP

Never hesitate to ask another teacher for help. I have discovered that some teachers claim they never need help, even though their classrooms may be in total chaos. It is usually the most confident teachers who ask for help. So quick, while you are new and humble and your ego allows you to admit when you need a hand, reach for it! Teachers love to help newer teachers, and you may learn someone else's "tricks of the trade" and use them in your classroom. Very often a teacher will be able to tell you just how to handle the girl who hums off-key just to annoy you or that boy who specializes in "snowing" teachers. I am sure that when you are experienced you will extend the same courtesy to some new protégé who is insecurely entering into our profession.

OBSERVING OTHER TEACHERS

You are new and will develop your own style, but it often takes a few years to learn what works and what doesn't. The first year you are sure to have both great successes and a few disappointments.

I have suggested that you ask other teachers for advice, and hopefully you will do that. To take it one step further, I suggest you ask your principal if you can observe another teacher, assuming it is all right with that teacher. Very often, you wonder why all the students love a particular teacher, and observing his style might help you refine your own.

TEACHER NEGATIVITY

As I visit new teachers, I hear a complaint that has me dismayed. They complain that some teachers are not happy in the profession and seem to criticize everything. Hopefully this doesn't happen too often, but I know it exists, especially from teachers who have burned out and are counting the days till retirement or from teachers who thought teaching would be an easy job. If by chance you are in the cafeteria where teachers are in the middle of a gripe session, take your lunch and move to a different table or find other enthusiastic teachers like yourself and dine together in someone's room. Negativity is contagious, but then again, so is enthusiasm. To veteran teachers, I ask you to share the positive experiences and help encourage the newbies to flourish.

JUST SAY NO

New teachers are wonderfully idealistic and often bite off more than they can chew. Couple that with a principal who needs a job done after every veteran teacher turned her down, and there you have it—the ingredients for a dismayed teacher, who just cannot say no.

The first year in the classroom is a lot different from your last year spent as a student teacher. You are now in charge of the class-room and the buck stops with you. Sometimes you just have to be able to say no. I have met many new teachers who are afraid to turn down their administrator's requests for fear they will think they are not good teachers. I have also met new teachers who believed they could do it all, only to find that grading papers and doing lesson plans can keep a teacher up into the wee hours of the morning.

I know it is not easy to say no, especially when you are so filled with energy and enthusiasm. I have seen too many teachers burn out in their first few years because they were overwhelmed by all they volunteered to do, not realizing that the everyday classroom respon-sibilities can take up to twice the amount of time they anticipated.

PART II

Beginning a Winning Year

Well, here you are, new and not-so-new teachers, ready to knock 'em dead! The beginning of every school year is always somewhat stressful because everyone is testing everyone else. Take a little time to ask yourself what you hope to accomplish this year, and then go ahead and make it happen!

CHAPTER TWO

They're Not Here Yet

GET TO SCHOOL EARLY

It is very important to get to school before the bell rings, especially if you are the teacher! Many of us actually have lives and often stay up late and crawl out of bed to get to school on time. Please try to get to your room at least a half hour before the kids. Drink some black coffee to make sure you are awake, and set up your room for the day. Have your lessons ready, have any materials needed at hand, and in general get yourself prepared for the day ahead. There is something comforting to kids when they enter the room and you are waiting to greet them. When we rush in panting, the day starts off on a more frenetic note and too often stays there.

ORGANIZING THE ROOM

Many teachers wait until their students arrive to decorate and fix up their rooms. It is always a good idea to make your room as welcoming as you can *before* they get there. Nothing is as foreboding to a young child, who may think school is a scary place, as a barren room without some "personality." You do not have to be an interior decorator, but it helps to have colored paper and some posters up that make your students feel comfortable. On the first day, you can give them a fun assignment about themselves and then put those papers up on the boards, so they feel like part of a group from day one.

Put Up Diplomas

What do you see in your doctor's office when you have a consultation with her? What do you see in your accountant's office when he is figuring out how to get you a huge refund? You see their diplomas proudly displayed. We are professionals and we have our diplomas as well, so why not display them? Of course our buildings are not secured, and it would be a disaster if your diploma was stolen. Why not make a copy, frame it, and display it behind your desk? Just a little touch for you to feel like the professional you are and perhaps serve as a reminder to parents who might forget.

Say Cheese

On the first day of school you might ask your students to bring in a recent photo of themselves for a project. You can make a collage or a rogue's gallery, and/or you can have them put their names underneath with a quote about themselves or you can do whatever creative idea you can come up with. A wonderful idea, though it is time consuming, is to ask the parents of your incoming students (if you know who they are) for photos of their children so these pictures will be visible to the students as soon as they walk in. This is especially appealing to young children who need something familiar to make them feel "at home."

It is fun to take a photo of each student at the end of the year and enclose the early picture with the end-of-the-year picture in a personal "Have a Great Summer" letter. Students will see how they have changed, and it is a nice way to end the year. However, you must make sure that you are allowed to take pictures of your students because some states do not permit it without parental consent.

Don't Be Caught Unprepared or Late

If you are unprepared and try to "wing it," the kids usually pick up on it. I have seen it happen when I had only part of a lesson mapped out and tried to fake the rest. In those instances, I would find myself losing the class because either I was looking for something, or my lesson had "lost its way," which is common when you are not sure of your material. Don't always count on your magnetic personality to hold their interest—it may let you down.

Being late is unconscionable for a teacher. In most states, a class cannot be left without a teacher because of the possible dangers to the students. Furthermore, as an educator you set the example. How hypocritical to punish your students for tardiness, while you stroll in at your leisure. None of this "Do as I say, not as I do" stuff works here.

Enthusiasm Is Caught, Not Taught

We want this year to be exciting and productive for our students as well as for ourselves. So first we have to psych ourselves to bubble with motivating enthusiasm. How do you accomplish that? Simple: You are well prepared, have the most exciting lessons ready to spark those eager minds, and realize that if you don't want to be there, neither will they. Tell them how you are looking forward to a great year together. You might even ask them what they expect from their teachers. (Of course, you will be everything they say and more!)

Friendly, But Not Buddies

In the beginning of the school year, a teacher is always being tested. That is when I tell my students, "My job is to teach, not to be a buddy." You don't want to be a pushover because kids can be merciless. I have seen teachers try to be "buddies" with their students. Believe it or not, that is not what your students want. They have their peers, and no matter how "cool" you are, you are not their pal.

I always tell kids who become too chummy that we can be friendly, but not friends. Too many teachers don't do this because they are afraid their students won't like them. Trust me, they will.

If you don't define the line, they get confused and may be disrespectful, and you, in turn, call a parent to complain about their disrespect. After I tell my students in my sternest voice that my job is to teach them, I smile and assure them they will adore me within a few weeks. (When I feel they're getting too chummy, I threaten them by telling them I will hang out with them and complain about my arthritis. That always does it!)

PERSONAL RECORDS DEBATE

You may find this unusual, and some teachers may disagree with me, but (except in the case of students with special needs) I do not read my students' academic/social record for a few weeks. I have found that reading comments from other teachers will slant the way I view a given student. You can tell me from today to tomorrow that the record won't affect how you perceive an individual, but take my word you will be prejudiced. If you hear, for instance, that a student is hostile, you will be anticipating it.

I know kids who did really fine work, although their records indicated that they were two years behind in reading. I had to fight myself not to lower my expectations. I am not suggesting you not read the records because it is clearly important for you to learn as much as you can about all of your students. I only encourage you to form your own opinions first.

This does not hold true for the medical part of the record. That should be looked at immediately. It is important for you to know right away if a student needs medication or has certain limitations. There was a boy in my third grade class who had a minor heart condition, and his physical activities had to be curtailed. Had I not read his record, I could have endangered his health because he would certainly be the last one to tell me he couldn't run 246 laps around the gymnasium. Most kids don't want to appear different from their peers.

You will, of course, keep this information confidential and never embarrass a child by referring to it unnecessarily, even in private.

CHAPTER THREE

They're Here

THE RUSH TO SEATS

I have a wonderful win-win solution to the awkward first-day rush to find seats. I let students sit where they choose; but as soon as they are seated, I explain that the seating arrangement is not permanent and will be changed. There might be a moan or two, but they usually accept that their seats are temporary. Live with the seating for a couple of days and if it seems to be working, tell them you trust their judgment and you will let them sit where they chose. Suddenly, you are considered the greatest teacher who ever lived because they feel you gave them something. If the seating arrangement has disruptive kids stimulated by other disruptive kids (or a student being intimidated by a nearby classmate), then you go back to your original deal. You are fair because you explained the plan up front, and their moaning will probably be kept to a minimum.

SEATING IDEAS

You can experiment with seating in many ways. There are simple ways, like seating by birthdays, by colors the students are wearing, or by reverse alphabetical order. You can even draw names out of a hat to show that the seating is random. But please don't seat by height or gender (see below).

Some people like to cluster their students while others prefer traditional rows. I personally prefer the horseshoe or the upside-down U. Basically, the class is in a semicircle, and I am in the front of the room. There is a trick to this structure that helps with discipline problems. When I first began, I thought I was really clever by putting the disruptive kids on both sides of the room rather than next to one another. *Don't do it!* They'll be facing one another—free to make faces, call out to each other, and act out every other possible human distraction. I finally learned to handle it by seating them all on one side, separated by more attentive students. The challenging kids cannot see one another and are more likely to focus on you. Another advantage is that you can be a physical presence either by standing close to inattentive students or by standing at opposite ends of the room and maintaining eye contact with anyone being disruptive.

If you have a class full of difficult students, I wouldn't try this seating plan; but if there is a good balance of students, this arrangement can get everyone involved in a positive way.

Something I strongly suggest is to rotate your students' seats. I used to do it once a month, and I made sure that they would be seated next to different students. When I did traditional rows, one row would move back a seat, and the next would move down one to assure that someone new was seating next to them. Socialization is very important, and students should be familiar with all their classmates rather than remain in the same cliques.

DON'T SEAT BY HEIGHT—OR GENDER

It is humiliating for the student who doesn't fit into his or her height "norm" to be singled out for this characteristic. Don't worry about the smaller kids—they can see from anywhere; and if they can't, they will let you know. The last thing a student wants is for you to focus on his or her lack of inches (or abundance thereof—tall kids can feel gawky, too!).

Lining up your students in size order is also not necessary. Try letting them line up by themselves or in alphabetical order (or reverse alphabetical order for those Zieglers who are always last).

Speaking of seating, why is it that we would never segregate children by race, yet we insist on segregating by gender? Even if it is what the students prefer, we as educators have got to stop perpetuating the

myth that males and females are "opposites." We have to foster interaction as early as possible and to not let each sex see the other one as
"the enemy" or "the other." Perhaps if we stop separating children by
gender in the earlier grades, boys and girls will become more enriched
by each other by the time they enter the middle grades.

DEALING FOR GROUPS

Using a deck of playing cards is a good strategy for assigning groups
when they don't have to be balanced by academic performance.
What I suggest is to try to make as many different combinations as
possible during the year, and that can be done simply enough by giving students playing cards and taping them to their book bags. (You
should jot down which card each student has so if one of them loses
his card, you have your own record.) If there are 28 students, you
hand out ace through 7 of all suits.

If you want a large group, you can call the suit. If you want small
groups, you can call the same number. If you want more than four,
you can pick two numbers. If you are ambitious and want to mix it
up, you can pick numbers and suits (red aces, black threes). There
are endless combinations. One of the advantages of this is that your
students will know early on that the grouping is random, and you
should also let them know that you will not tolerate groaning if a
student they don't like joins the group.

RECORD KEEPING QUESTIONNAIRE

You will need lots of information from your students and their
parents. A good idea is to have a questionnaire ready for them to
fill out along with one for their parents. You should include your
students' names, addresses, phone numbers, and e-mail addresses
along with their schedules so you can find them in the event that you
need to reach them. You can ask for their extracurricular activities
and find out if they work after school. Parents should give you their
work phone numbers and their availability during the day. You can
ask parents if they have any skills they would be willing to share
with your class. It is also a good idea to ask what language is spoken
at home. You might also include a question about things that parents

want to ask you. Giving parents an opportunity to ask you questions in advance of parent teacher conferences might enable you to give them thoughtful answers. You might even offer suggestion questions such as "Have you noticed any behavioral changes? What can we do together to make sure my child has a great year?"

When you have all this information returned to you, put it in a large binder; and if you are feeling particularly organized that week, you might buy tab pages that have pockets in them. Now you have a binder with every student's name and pertinent information. Keep conference notes, conversations with parents and counselors, referral slips, and so on in this binder; therefore, everything will be organized and easy to find if you need to refer to it.

NOW AND LATER CARDS

Now and Later Cards first introduce the students to you at the beginning of the year and later show how they have changed by the end of the year.

You begin by giving out small index cards and composing questions that will give you insight about your students. Examples might include the following:

What is your favorite subject?

What is your pet peeve?

What do you hope will happen to you this year?

What music do you like?

Save the cards and on the last day of school, return the cards to them. They always laugh because half of the answers hardly describe them at the end of the year. I have seen teens cringe because they liked the "wrong" rock group in September and can't believe how uncool they were.

THE FIRST DAY "SNEAKER"

A wonderful first day activity for younger children is to place an array of materials on each student's desk. The packet holding the materials could be in the shape of a sneaker and called "Stepping Into the Fifth Grade Sneaker." Having simple tasks on their desks lets them get started without having to ask for directions, gives them something to do right away, and hopefully sets the tone for the rest of the year. To make it really special, you can write each student's name on his or her "sneaker."

FUN INTRODUCTIONS

Depending on the age of your students, there are many ways they can introduce themselves. I'll just throw a few at you.

Younger children can say their names and add a noun, as in "Sarah the Singer." When you do this, please don't make children repeat all the names said before them. This is very stressful to kids and unfair to the last child. Another way is to have kids reveal one thing that is special about them (or makes them different from others in your class). Students can pair up and find out as much as they can about one another and then introduce their partners. Some students simply find it is easier to talk about others rather than about themselves. This exercise might be easier if you have a prepared list of suggested questions. Another pairing strategy is to have each two-some list a few things they have in common and a few ways in which they are totally different from one another. If there is an odd number of students, go ahead and jump in and be the other half of a pair. A really fun exercise is to have each child write one truth about himself and one lie and have the class guess which is which. It's a good ice-breaker because the kids love it and it is easy for you to take part. If you feel more comfortable with traditional methods, you can give them a written assignment wherein they introduce themselves on paper and read what they wrote aloud. This is also a subtle way to assess their writing skills.

PUT YOUR NAME—AND PHONE NUMBER?—ON THE BOARD

Needless to say, your name goes on the board *first thing*. Since you are the boss, it's really important that they know who you are. But you're probably asking, "Why in heaven's name would I give these total strangers my home phone number?" You probably have visions of half the school calling and asking if your refrigerator is running and then telling you to go catch it! There may be those who would actually do that, but the amazing discovery I've made is that when they have permission to call, they usually don't unless it is school related.

I do this for two reasons. First, they feel it is such an act of trust that you would actually let them call you at home. I make it very clear that they may call only if it is very important and they must speak to me. They may not call about homework assignments because they have a homework buddy for that. (See Homework Buddies on page 43.) I also explain that I go to bed early and not to call after 9 o'clock. Second, I am so generous with my number because if they wanted to make a prank call, all they'd have to do is look my number up in the phone book!

In the beginning there are usually a few kids who will call on a pretense just to hear my "at-home" voice. Occasionally, I've gotten calls from kids in crisis. Very seldom did I get "mystery calls," and the few that I did get may have been students or just people dialing a wrong number and not using proper phone etiquette.

This is just my experience. Many teachers are not comfortable with this and therefore should not do it. (It's easy not to if your name is Smith!)

YOU'VE GOT MAIL

Okay, so you do not want to give your students your telephone number. However, there is another way to communicate with them outside of school—through the Internet. Now that most schools have an e-mail address for each teacher, your students and their parents can ask you questions or express concerns and you can respond in 100 words or less.

Some teachers give their students their personal e-mail address, but let me warn you what can happen if you are on their buddy list. You suddenly hear the ping of an "instant message," and then another and then another, and suddenly you are aware that your entire class wants to chat online. Consider using a different screen name so all you have to do is switch your screen name and your students will not know that you are surfing the Net planning your vacation.

TANGIBLE CLASS GUIDELINES AND RULES

It is important that you think through what you expect from your class and what they should expect from you. You can explain everything to them in detail, but it helps to have the rules in writing and in their hands (and on the bulletin board). You can give them two sets. The first must be kept in their notebooks, and the other they and their parents must sign and return to you to keep on file. During the year, when a student says, "I didn't know you would fail me because I didn't do 188 homework assignments," you can pull out her signed agreement. It is important that the parents sign this agreement because some parents have been known to try to put teachers on the defensive, saying they were not informed of certain requirements their child had to fulfill. You can show them the signed contract and this usually ends the confrontation.

LET STUDENTS SET RULES AND CONSEQUENCES

You can ask the class what rules they consider fair. (Don't ask what rules they think are unfair—if you do, you'll be sorry!)

For instance, I ask them what would make a classroom feel safe, and then we brainstorm and compile a list of rules. It is hard for them to complain that the rules they set are unfair.

Of course, if you see that they are not being serious and are making rules such as "There should be no homework ever," go back to a dictatorship and declare yourself czar.

YOU OWN THE LIMELIGHT

The beginning of the school year is the time to establish yourself as the person in charge.

Observe how peer groups form and how you sometimes unwittingly become part of this process. I have seen some kids be perceived as "cool" if they can put down the teacher. If they are successful, you're in big trouble. Common behavior patterns of this kind of student are to yell out to the teacher, mutter under his breath, or just engage other kids in a conversation while you are right there at the front of the room being just as nice as you can be. What to do?

Sometimes a quick glance at the disruptive student may suffice. If not, you may have to do the unthinkable, and that might involve embarrassing the student. Stop and explain to the "cool" kid that under no circumstances do you talk over anyone else and that you will protect that right for everyone in the room. (To some, this can be terribly intimidating.)

If you talk over a conversation, the noise level just rises; and before you know it, no one can be heard and you are yelling. I am not saying that a classroom should always be quiet—I would hardly want that—but when the lesson is teacher directed, the teacher has the floor.

Good educational experiences usually encourage enthusiastic talking, and that is music to the ears.

You Can Always Ease Up

It is tempting to be permissive from the beginning because no one wants to start out the year with all those "mean" rules. But unless you establish them early on, you will pay the consequences. If you say there will be homework every day, they will groan but expect it. On the day you give them no homework, you'll be seen as a saint.

But the reverse can be catastrophic. Try telling kids you won't give them homework on the weekends and then do just the opposite. You will have a potential student revolution on your hands.

Sit With Your Students

Too often we stand in front of the room and just lecture. It can be boring and sometimes even a little intimidating; but alas, that's where the blackboard or the overhead is, and standing there brings the focus to you. But on occasion, I pull up a chair and sit with my students, usually while reading a story or having a class discussion. Sitting at their level makes everyone feel more comfortable. I have found that this strategy encourages more students to participate.

Also, sitting on top of a desk, rather than standing, accomplishes the same thing and puts off your need to purchase those less attractive "sensible shoes."

GREET STUDENTS AT THE DOOR

Very often our students feel alienated in school, especially older students who travel from teacher to teacher. They are often one of hundreds of students in a building and rarely get individual recognition unless they are outstanding in some way.

Teachers should always be ready to teach and be waiting for their students. Why not greet them at the door? What is really special is greeting them by name. One colleague of mine who taught ninth graders would refer to his students by their surnames, which made them feel they were treated like respected adults.

DOCUMENT! DOCUMENT! DOCUMENT!

When there is an accident or a major infraction, teachers must put it in writing and on record. Make sure your statements are nonjudgmental and contain only the facts without personal interpretation.

Sometimes, because we are so overwhelmed with all our responsibilities as a teacher, we put off writing the report and forget about it. Try not to. Very often parents will side with their child no matter what and will accuse you of picking on the student. It is helpful if a teacher is able to retrieve a file and show parents that the child has past offenses that are documented. According to law, you must document accidents because lawsuits are becoming increasingly common. Basically, I am just telling you to protect yourself.

I had this horrendously disruptive and hurtful child in my class. When I spoke to the mother, she initially expressed concern. As time went by her concern shifted to "getting the teachers" rather than getting help for her son. He had set a fire in the bathroom, and all she wanted to see was the documentation. Rather than address the serious issues regarding her son's behavior, she would put me on the defensive. I was stunned to see how few teachers had written up reports on him (though we would share "Jimmy" stories over lunch, trying to find solutions to help him). This mother attacked me verbally, saying I just didn't like her child. (More about those parents later.) Had I had all the documentation, I might have been able to get this child help. He eventually ended up getting hurt by another student instead of getting the counseling he desperately needed.

YOWKS! FIVE MINUTES LEFT

It was bound to happen. You had it perfectly planned—a 40-minute lesson for your 30-minute time slot. But guess what? It bombed! You lost their interest, you tried every trick in the book to resuscitate your lesson, and you found that you still had time to spare. Not enough time to start something new, but too much time to sit and wait for the bell to ring.

What to do? I don't care what grade you're teaching: Play Simon Says. It's a sure crowd pleaser. If you want to be more cerebral, play Hangman, and to make sure they enjoy it, divide the room in half and make it a team competition. My Hangman game is always a sentence rather than a word. (It depends on how many minutes you have left to ad lib!) Reading a story that can be picked up at any point is another good idea. You know you have a winner when the bell rings and they groan.

END THE FIRST DAY ON AN UP NOTE

Make sure the day ends on a positive note. You may have told them about the term projects they will be getting and given them lots of books to take home to cover. But today you can be so kind by announcing that they will have only a short assignment because you want them to be well rested for a great day tomorrow. Your day ends, hopefully, with smiling students who feel you are the fairest person in the world and who will be indebted to you forever—Okay, maybe not forever, but a few hours are better than nothing!

CHAPTER FOUR

They're Gone and You Survived!

EVERYTHING CAN BE REDONE

Even before your students come in, keep in mind that nothing you do or say is written in stone. You may have great strategies that you just know will work, but suddenly you find everything you said and did bombed! Don't fret. Tomorrow is another day, and you can redo whatever has to be redone. If your students give you the "But you said yesterday" routine, explain to them you were not happy with the results and that one good thing about being the teacher is that you can change what you think needs to be modified. Period!

YOU'RE NOT A SHRINK

During the day you may have encountered a student who you are sure belongs anywhere but in your class. Remember, unless you are a trained counselor or therapist, you must know your professional and legal limitations. We all have students who create trouble for themselves and for others. If their behavior concerns you, I strongly suggest that you refer them to the school guidance counselor, who is trained to deal with these issues. If you have students writing journals or if you are told something in confidence that you think needs professional attention, you may have to betray that student's confidence (see Journals on page 112). Students may talk about suicide, abuse, drugs, depression, or other serious matters that require a professional. You are a teacher, not a counselor. It is better to betray a confidence than to risk a child harming herself because your judgment was wrong.

Don't Take Their Behavior Personally

As wonderful as you are, their peers' opinions are the ones that really count. I have had students ask if they could stay around and chat with me after school, only to ignore me the next day when they were among their friends. How could they like me so much at 3:00 p.m. on Monday and ignore me at 9:00 a.m. on Tuesday? Easy, their friends are more important. Don't panic. They'll be back, and hopefully you will greet them with open arms because you are the one who makes them feel safe and helps them learn.

You Can't Win 'Em All

If you are the sensitive type, you feel disappointed when your students don't like you or the lesson on which you worked so hard. It is important not to take things personally because most times they are not personal, although on occasion they are. Some may think your approach to teaching is the pits and may think your style was created to put them to sleep (see Am I Boring? on page 59). Well, that does happen, and unless most of your students feel that way, I wouldn't worry. If most of your students manage to stay awake, learn, and even miraculously laugh at your jokes, just enjoy the feat of pleasing most. You can't please everyone.

Go Home and Chill Out

My daughter joined me at one of my student teacher seminars. At the time she was a seasoned teacher of six months. (She was actually nominated for Teacher of the Year in her high school during that time—Okay, I am bragging, but I am a mother!) Her advice to the new teachers was to go home after they finished their first week and just indulge themselves. She suggested they take a bubble bath, read a book with absolutely no redeeming value, or just go to the movies with friends. She encouraged them to divorce themselves from the job for a little while. I had forgotten how consuming it could be, and from the smiles in the audience, I knew she totally understood where they were coming from. I think that is wonderful advice for even the most seasoned veteran.

PART III

Helping Students Be Responsible

Our students desperately need order in their lives, and it is up to us to help them by setting limits with them. Limits make them feel safe. When we define limits, we are telling our students they cannot venture into water that is too deep. Our students often seem to be irresponsible, so we have to gently show them that every action has a consequence. Following are some strategies that help them assume responsibility as you set well-defined limits with clear consequences.

CHAPTER FIVE

Establishing Routines

CREATURES OF HABIT

I want to stress here the need for routines. This goes for you as well as for your students. Schoolchildren are creatures of habit and work beautifully when they know what is expected of them. When they enter my classroom, it is a given that they take their seats as attendance is being taken. Other teachers might allow their students to mill around for a few minutes, but in either case the students know what is expected of them. Homework, classroom chores, and certain structured lessons can easily be "routinized." You will find that routines provide you with extra time for constructive teaching instead of spending time giving unnecessary explanations.

THE STANDARDIZED NOTEBOOK

I make all my older students buy a large three-ring binder. I have had more confrontations than I would like with eager students who bought small, two-hole books with reams of nonstandard-sized paper. These are usually those students who can least afford it and who make me seem like the Wicked Witch of the West.

The reality is that small paper is bothersome to grade because it usually falls somewhere under the desk and most teacher handouts are on standard 8 1/2-by-11-inch paper, which students cannot put in their notebooks because they don't fit. They simply fold them up neatly . . . and they are never seen again.

THE "DO NOW" OR "WARM UP"

Teachers have been doing the "Do Now" exercise for centuries. The idea is to have a short exercise prepared for students to do as soon as they walk into the room. It sets the tone for learning from the minute they enter. It should be something relatively easy and should not take more than a few minutes. (For older students it could be called "Warm Up.")

An example of a Do Now is to have a quote on the board, like the contents of a Hallmark greeting card or a thought-provoking quote such as, "The only time you should look down at someone is when you are helping him or her up." All the students have to do is copy it and write about what it means and how it relates to them. (They need not use a new sheet of paper each time but rather just date each entry and continue from the previous "Do Now.") When they've completed the exercise, spend a few more minutes sharing some of their writings with the whole class. In those five minutes, the class has gotten settled, notebooks have been opened, and pens are poised for working. Pretty shrewd, huh?

THE AIM OF "AIM"

I also put the aim for every lesson on the board. It focuses on exactly what you intend to teach. We want our students to come in and settle down right away so that we can begin our activity. When my students walk into the room, they automatically look at the board for the "Do Now" and then for the "Aim," which they write down in their notebooks. They know the business of the day, and it is a settling routine. They also look for the homework assignment in its usual place on the board. I have had students indignantly reprimand me for not having the "Aim" on the board!

CLASS WRAP-UPS

A nice touch is to give closure to your lessons. You may ask your students what they liked best, what they learned, what they didn't like, or any other comments relevant to the lesson. This is not meant to be an informal quiz but rather a closing discussion on what was accomplished during that period.

I would often tell my students how I felt the lesson went, and sometimes I had to break the news that teachers do not corner the market on being boring. If a class was notably unresponsive or inattentive, I would inform them that they did not participate enough and I found *them* bor-r-r-ing. (But keep a smile on your face so they know you are teasing in a good-natured way.)

WHEN TO GIVE OUT WORKSHEETS

Okay, you have spent hours on a worksheet, but you know there are parts that need to be explained before your students can begin their task. You give the sheet to them right away and tell them not to look at it until you have finished your instruction. Well, that's like giving a beautifully wrapped birthday gift to a child and telling her not to look at it for a few days. Don't count on it!

If students need the sheet for clarification, make sure you get them into the habit of having everyone look at the same place on the paper at the same time. Some will say they didn't hear you explain the rules, but you and I know why. They were reading ahead!

YOU TEACH, NOT VIDEOS

Today there are so many wonderful instructional materials on video. Sometimes it is so tempting to let the video do the teaching, but you are the one getting paid. Too often we are tempted to sit back and let the kids see a book on video rather than read the book. I am not saying videos are not appropriate. *After* reading a book, bringing it to life through film can be very exciting and should be perceived as a treat. Using them too often just perpetuates a problem we are seeing more and more—too many of our kids are glued to a little screen, and I sometimes fear they are losing the ability to conceptualize. I am not saying videos are unsuitable for the classroom; I am just cautioning you that the number should be limited. I have seen parents and administrators complain when this becomes a pattern, and the teacher develops a reputation as a slacker.

Who Dismisses?

In school or grades in which there are departmentalized classes, a bell usually rings to signal that the period is over. I have my students exercise self-control when the bell rings. They have to wait for *me* to tell them they are dismissed. If I am explaining something when the bell rings, the moment will be lost if I am left standing there babbling to any emptying classroom. Experience has taught me to let them know that "I dismiss, not the bell."

It takes time for them to stop instinctively jumping up and rushing out of my room, but this is a rule that I expect them to respect. It is also an excellent lesson in self-control. Of course, you must be sure to leave enough time for students to get to their next class promptly.

CHAPTER SIX

Have Them Come (and Stay) Prepared

YOU ARE NOT THE SUPPLY STORE

There are students who choose not to bring a pen or pencil to school and who always seem to be out of notebook paper. Their rulers and other necessary school supplies are always missing. The easy way out is to hand these kids pens, paper, and so forth. *Don't!* That is not your job. Many teachers tell me it is just easier to give them pencils, but in my opinion, that is just enabling them to be irresponsible. They may end up not doing work because they have nothing to write with or on. Well, that is a consequence of not being prepared.

Before you think I'm too stingy or harsh, I have to stress again that you must know your audience. If his pen runs out of ink or if she has no more paper because she just used her last sheet, that is a different story. But even that has to have a small consequence, and so I suggest the next hint.

"YOU OWE ME A FAVOR"

If you want to lend a pen or pencil to a student, tell her that you will lend her a pencil, but she will owe you a favor, such as straightening the desks, erasing the boards, sorting the books, and so on. It is up to you. Just jot their names down and I am sure you can think of some chore for them to do. If it is a chore they don't like doing, they might think twice before coming to school unprepared.

BLESS THE BARGAIN STORES

I have suggested a standard three-hole loose-leaf book that makes it easier for your students to keep their papers together. If you teach in an area where money is scarce, you might go to Staples or Costco or any discount store to pick up binders for them. Many of these places will give teachers an additional discount if they can produce ID. You can ask your students to bring in a dollar, and you can give them a binder and change to boot. If you teach the lower grades, you can buy them in different colors and have them use markers to decorate and make each one truly unique. It is also a good idea to buy a few extras because there are always one or two binders that get "eaten by the dog."

COLLATERAL, PLEASE

Before I lend students a pen, pencil, ruler, or some other such supply, I ask for collateral. I have gotten earrings, dimes, bus passes, wallets, and hats. At the end of the class, they return what they borrowed and I return their collateral.

Please be careful not to take keys as collateral. Once a girl forgot to return my pen, I still had her key, and she was locked out of her house. Some teachers ask for a shoe, but I don't suggest this either because students may find this humiliating. But small tokens as collateral reinforce that we don't get things for nothing, nor should we expect that.

If your school has ID tags for the students, that might be good collateral because they need them and will notice them missing. This should bring them back to your room with pencil in hand.

I will admit during my career I have amassed two Knicks hats, $1.30, and two earrings that were forgotten. Who says teachers are underpaid?

STRINGS ATTACHED

When I first heard this I just couldn't stop laughing at the visual, so let me share it with you. A woman told us that her husband was a carpenter and that he screwed an eyehook into a brick and then tied a pencil to it. She had three bricks lined up on the counter, and if a student needed a pencil, he had to take the brick and all. Can you visualize this without smiling? Someone e-mailed me and told me he didn't have a brick, and with great pride he told me he used a hubcap. We don't have to be so extreme, but attaching a pencil to a larger object might be a sure way to get it back.

CREATIVE PENCILS

I have pencils that are huge and are topped off with funny looking orange haired heads and a few with gaudy sequined flowers. No one else has these pencils and most kids don't want to walk around with them, especially if they are older. (And boys would die before walking around with anything sequined.) If a student removes it from your room, it is easily identifiable and assures you a quick return. Many teachers buy personalized pencils so there is no question to whom it belongs.

Another surefire way to discourage them from asking you for a pencil is to give them a golf pencil. THEY HATE THEM! They are small, do not have erasers, and are awkward to write with. I can't tell you how many students complained about these pencils and were quite annoyed that I would supply them with something so "unacceptable." I had to gently remind them that it is their responsibility to bring their perfect writing tool to school, not mine. If they don't like it, they can bring their own. We just can't make it too comfortable for them.

THE SHARPENER COVER

Children asking to sharpen pencils is something that can easily drive a teacher crazy. A teacher told me she put a cover on the sharpener after a designated period of time. She put it on after the class had a chance to sharpen the pencils, and it served as a visual reminder that the sharpener was unavailable. She wrote the words, "Sharpener Asleep" on the cover. For older children, just putting a cover over it denotes the sharpener is off limits.

PENCILS = CHARITY

Who knows, you might be lucky and have a school that actually gives you pencils. A nice idea is to sell pencils to your unprepared students at a slight profit and tell them that the surplus money will be donated to a charity at the end of the school year. What is nice about this is that it opens a discussion about charity and becomes a class project. You might have several groups do some research on a particular charity and have them present it to the class. Then the class can vote. It is also a wonderful opportunity for them to discuss charities with their parents. One note of caution, make sure it is acceptable school policy.

SWAPPING

Very often a student's pencil point breaks and you already have the sharpener off limits. What one can do is have a bucket with sharpened pencils in it. All your student has to do is put his pencil in the bucket and take out a sharpened one. This way there is no noisy sharpener to disturb the class, and it is quick and painless. The nice thing is that it ties in with the rule, "You Owe Me a Favor." The student who came unprepared and to whom you gave a pencil now owes you a favor. That favor is to sharpen the pencils and replenish the bucket with good pointy pencils for those who did come prepared.

SCRAP PAPER

Have you noticed that doodling seems to be a national pastime in your classroom? I have seen so many kids run out of paper because they have "doodled" on all the blank pages in their notebooks. Kids will waste paper often because they didn't like the way they wrote a word, so they discard it. A good idea is to have a scrap paper box.

When kids come up to you complaining they have nothing to write on, tell them to go to the scrap box where one side of the paper has no writing on it. They may not like that because they like perfect paper, but it might teach a lesson in not wasting paper and to make sure that they have more than enough when they come to school.

CHAPTER SEVEN

Homework Strategies

THE IMPORTANCE OF HOMEWORK

Believe it or not, your students understand that homework is a sign that a teacher cares about them. It is easier not to give homework, but we must give challenging assignments. Of equal importance is the manner in which the assignments are treated by the teacher. Are the homework assignments checked? Marked? Discussed? Used in a follow-up lesson?

Homework is also a parent-teacher relationship tool. The homework represents you. Make sure it isn't just busywork, or so difficult that you expect parents to play a major role in it. (See Parents and Homework on page 147.)

THE HOMEWORK SPOT

It is a good idea to have a short daily homework assignment prepared from Day 1. They'll groan, but don't be put off by it. They expect homework! I always put my assignments in the same spot on the board. When my students walk into my room, they automatically look at the upper left-hand corner of the board. It just makes for an easy routine, and homework becomes something they expect—and should get!

Numbering Homework

I always prefer to place my homework assignments in the upper left-hand corner of the board with the date and the assignment number. I ask a student to copy the date, the assignment, and its number, and post it on a sheet of paper on a bulletin board. When a student misses a homework assignment, all she has to do is look at the sheet and there is the date and the number of the missed assignment.

Often you might have to explain the lesson one-on-one so that the student will be able to do the homework. For example, if the assignment is to write a haiku and the student was absent for that lesson, the assignment per se doesn't mean much without an explanation.

Collecting Homework

Collecting homework can be a time-consuming activity, and we want to save every moment for instruction. To save time, I have large manila envelopes tacked up on bulletin boards. I have students drop the homework assignment into the envelope that has their class or the appropriate subject written on the front, and I collect their work at the end of the day. Ideally, you should collect the homework near your desk so you can write down who is unprepared while the class is quietly working on the "Do Now" assignment. The following strategy is ideal if you find that writing down the names is too time consuming.

Hand In a Blank Sheet

When you collect homework, rather than ask who didn't do it and then writing it in your grading book, just ask your students to pass in the homework. You explain to the class that you want everyone to pass in the assignment and if they didn't do it, to just hand in a blank paper with their name, signature, and date on it. If you want, you can allow them to write the reason they didn't do the homework. This serves two purposes: it is a quick way to see who didn't do homework, and the best reason is that you now have documentation. So when parents insist their children did their homework or tell you that their child said you didn't give them any homework, you now have their blank papers dated and signed as proof.

SIGN ON THE DOTTED LINE

It always happens. There are some students who do not hand in their projects and have a million excuses for not doing so. By this time you should have made it very clear that you rarely accept any excuse as long as your students are able to walk in with both arms intact. I have an excellent strategy to get them to take these projects more seriously.

One day my daughter visited me with a batch of class work she had to grade. Among the projects, I noticed several Day-Glo papers sticking out and asked her why they were there. She explained that those who did not hand in their projects were given one of these papers. On it was written, "I, *(student's name),* have *CHOSEN* not to do this assigned project and understand the consequences." They had to read it, sign it, and date it. Your student now sees you with tangible evidence of her lack of responsibility, and the vivid color stands out. It also serves as documentation if you need to show parents why their child did poorly in your class.

HOMEWORK BUDDIES

In Put Your Name—and Phone Number?—on the Board (page 19), I suggested you give your students your telephone number. If you were brave enough to do so, I suggest you strongly stress that they may not call you for a homework assignment. That is not your job. You do that during the day, and at night you are entitled to your privacy unless they have an urgent need to speak to you.

To eliminate the problem of missed homework, I have them take the phone numbers and e-mail addresses of the two people seated near them. (Make sure they are not their best friends because they already *have* that information.) If a student is absent, he has contact information for at least two classmates who know the assignments and, therefore, has no excuse for missing any homework. Hopefully, they can find the homework that you've put on the Internet.

H-O-M-E-W-O-R-K

This one is fun for students and is a great motivator to do homework. I put the word H-O-M-E-W-O-R-K on the board. Each time the entire class did the homework assignment, I would erase a letter. When the entire word was erased, I would give them a pizza party. You can tell my class didn't all do their homework that often, or else I would have ended up in the poor house. For teachers who have students who usually hand in their work, the reward might be NO HOMEWORK for a day or some free time. I am sure you can think of your own reward that isn't too hard on your wallet.

OOPS PASS

At the beginning of the year you can make up an "oops pass." (The number is up to you, but one or two is suggested, no more.) This is a free pass for students who, for whatever reason, miss a homework assignment. (If you are a Monopoly player, you can call this strategy, "Get out of homework free.") Sometimes a student on a rare occasion misses a homework assignment, and giving him a free pass once or twice a year makes you seem fair and understanding. These passes are of little use to the chronic homework evader, but it works for the students who are more conscientious. You also explain that if they don't use them, they can trade them in at the end of the year for some reward or some honor. You will be surprised at how many students don't use them.

You also should explain to your students that the pass cannot be used for every homework assignment, as there are some that must be handed in. Remind them of movie theaters that have signs on the window when there is a special movie playing . . . "No passes allowed for this performance." You can do the same with the special homework, but make sure you mention that passes won't be accepted at the time of the assignment.

HOMEWORK PENALTY (WITH ROOM FOR REDEMPTION)

Homework is the responsibility of the student, plain and simple. In most cases the student has a choice whether to do it or not. If a homework assignment is not done, the student may get a −2. At the end of the term when we confer (see Confer for Grades on page 56),

I add up all the minuses and deduct them from the student's grade average. On occasion a student might fail my class even though she passed exams.

Before you call me heartless, read on. I allow students to make up the missing homework within a short period of time—let's say two days. When they make it up, I give them back 1 1/2 points. Now they lose only half a point, which may not add up to very much, but this still teaches them that there is a consequence.

HOMEWORK HELPER . . . YOU!

I spent much of my career working with students with specials needs. Many of their needs were not necessarily qualifiers for special education, but rather their needs were a lack of self-confidence or a lack of parental support. Very often parents are overwhelmed and do not know how to help their children with their homework. Sometimes kids are just so disorganized that they don't know where to begin and how to end.

If you have a bunch of kids who need some help with homework, I suggest you allow about five minutes before the end of the day or the end of your class to get them started. Sometimes when students are disorganized they become almost paralyzed and can't get started on their homework. In five minutes you can get them started, and odds are they will bring in their completed homework. It is a great time investment. Not all students need this help, and for them it is a perk since they will have started their homework and have more time to play video games at home.

CHAPTER EIGHT

Bathroom Breaks

THE SIGN-OUT BOOK

I hate to be responsible for someone else's bodily functions—it just gives me too much power! When students approach me bobbing up and down, I feel terribly guilty saying they may not leave the room. So I let them be responsible for monitoring their own bathroom habits.

I have a sheet on which they sign their names and write the time and date when they leave the room. I assure them that I trust they are not just leaving the room because I am a bore. However, I do check the sheet, and I can tell at a glance which students are abusing the privilege. I will discuss this issue with these students privately, showing them how often they are leaving the room and how they are taking advantage of my trust, and I will question whether they are being responsible or if they have a medical problem I must report. As a result, they tend to leave the room less often because they know I check the sign-out sheets.

"CAN YOU WAIT A MINUTE?"

This is so simple and so effective. This is one of those ideas that works and I can't explain exactly why. When a student walks into the room, he suddenly realizes he has to go to the bathroom . . . immediately! Just ask, "Can you wait a minute?" Most times he will notice that the urge dissipates and he won't ask you again (probably because he didn't have to go in the first place). Of course, if he is still squirming, don't take a chance and of course let him go.

THE VISUAL PASS

There are some teachers who allow their students to leave the room whenever they ask to use the bathroom. If you don't want to be bothered by their asking to leave, you might have two cups attached to the wall or to a bulletin board. One cup will say boys and the other girls (or male/female depending on the age). In each cup you put a tongue depressor that will serve as the pass. If they see there is a tongue depressor in the cup, they know they may leave. This way, you never have more than two out of your room and they can see in a minute if the pass is available. Please promise me, however, that you will not paint the cups blue and pink!

SECRET CODE

Nothing is more disheartening than when you are into a great teacher moment, where the class is awake and enthralled by your every word, when you ask a question the waving hands are blinding you . . . and then you call on a student and you hear, "May I go to the bathroom?" THUD!

What you might teach your class from day one is a secret code when they raise their hands for permission to use the bathroom. You can teach the class to cross their fingers if they are asking to go to the bathroom so that you don't call on a student who has no idea what the answer is. This way you can visually spot the student who wants to leave your room. You can signal a yes or a no immediately by one look or nod.

BATHROOM COUPONS

A good way to limit the number of times a student leaves the room is to start them off at the beginning of the year with four bathroom coupons. They may use them to leave the room when they must, thus eliminating disrupting a lesson. You can print these passes at the beginning of the year, and they redeem them by signing and dating each one as they are used and placing it in a box for that purpose.

What often happens is that the students save them because they never know when they are going to need them, and they have two or three left over at the end of the year. You might mention that those passes not used can be turned in at the end of the year and redeemed for something special.

RESPECTING THE RESTROOM

This strategy, when it was first suggested to me, really surprised me, and I pooh-poohed it. Our girls' bathroom was absolutely disgusting. The girls would write on the walls, throw trash around, and mark the mirrors with lipstick. The custodians were up in arms and with good reason. One of the new teachers suggested letting the girls decorate the bathroom. She assured me it would make a difference. We got a committee together, including the custodians, and discussed how to make the restroom a place that shows respect for the users. To make a long story short, they painted it a pretty color, and the artistic students painted a mural with the help of the art teacher. I had to humbly admit to her that my skepticism was wrong. The bathroom was never trashed and to atone for my skepticism, I brought in silk flowers that stayed in that bathroom for the entire year.

THAT TIME OF THE MONTH

Women and men reading this will probably have different reactions.

When a girl asks her teacher if she can get a sanitary napkin or tampon, how can anyone say no? It's easy—once you discover she has her period 29 out of 30 days of the month with different teachers.

Also, men sometimes fall prey to the "I can't do any work . . . it's that time of the month" complaint, as a young girl's face contorts in agony. Guys: Don't be a pushover—be a little suspicious. Because men don't menstruate, they believe the worst. In some cases, young women *do have* bad cramps, and if this pattern is apparent, you should refer her to the school nurse because she may have a serious problem. (Male teachers might ask a female colleague to assess the situation.)

But we must not treat menstruation as a disability. If we do, women will not have a fair shot in the real world if they are "disabled" for a few days every month. Because I am a woman, I am able to talk more freely with my girls. I have had girls ask to go home because they have their periods, and I would whisper that I also have mine, but I will stick out the day and I know they can too. Menstruation is a natural part of life and should be treated as such. There are many painkillers that can alleviate cramps, but again I must stress that if a student is in obvious pain, you must make sure her parents are informed, and you should bring her to the school nurse for evaluation.

CHAPTER NINE

Empowering Students

WE MAKE OUR OWN CHOICES

Our students have to learn that they have choices—we all have choices. Some are easy and some are more difficult. I talk a great deal about consequences. A belief that I hold dear is that every act has a consequence, and that our actions determine how we will live our lives.

I remember a terrific student of mine who was caught threatening other students to give him their homework. He claimed he did it because he was broke and had to work after school, so he didn't have time to do his homework. I pointed out that there were many other students working after school who did not choose to cheat. It was his choice, and he chose to intimidate others and then to portray himself as the victim.

I totally empathized with his problems, but I would not enable him by sanctioning his actions. Too often, teachers feel sorry for students and let things like that slide. I feel that doing that is an injustice, and we have to be tough for the sake of those very children about whom we care so much.

THE RIGHT TO PASS

Were you one of those kids who dreaded having to read aloud in class? I was. I would count the number of people before me and try to find the paragraph I would have to read and then practice it over and over in my head. By the time it was my turn to read, I thought I was going to have an anxiety attack. I feared making a mistake and having others laugh at me.

To ease this anxiety in your students, give them the right to pass. Once the classroom is safe, you will find that these "passers" will eventually partake in class discussions.

If I find that a student is not participating at all, I have to modify the passing rule. I engage her in a discussion in which there can be no wrong answer. It may be something as simple as "What is your favorite holiday?" If she continues to pass, I'll say, "Come on, please share that with us." I then pick up on the theme and ask follow-up questions about what she does on that holiday, and so forth. In short, getting students to talk about something with which they are familiar initiates them into the world of oral communication in a relatively nonthreatening way.

The Sanctuary

This strategy is a powerful one, and I have received tons of notes thanking me for sharing it. I explain to my students that my classroom is a sanctuary. They must define the word ("a safe place"). Then we brainstorm answers to the question, "What makes a classroom safe?" The resulting list is put on the bulletin board and must be respected. When someone hurts someone else's feelings, I stop immediately and ask, "What is this classroom called?" They will say, "It is a sanctuary." I keep doing this until they pick it up and say to each other, "Hey, quiet! This is a sanctuary." I never thought it would take effect as well as it did, but the students valued the safe feeling they had in the room. At first it was a joke, but then it became a source of comfort. Children who in the past would never read aloud would do so now because they knew no one would make fun of them if they made a mistake. In order for this to be effective, you must teach the "Tacit Approval" strategy below. This strategy works for all grade levels.

Tacit Approval

In order to make your classroom a "sanctuary," your students must be armed with ways to deal with the bullies without being confrontational.

As I mentioned earlier, several of my classes, particularly the ones on prejudice awareness and sex education, required a very "safe" classroom because of the course contents. But how can students feel safe enough to share personal experiences and feelings if they fear being made fun of by their peers?

I write the words *Tacit Approval* on the board and define the term as unspoken approval. Examples of tacit approval can be snickering, pointing, and winking.

For example, we all know that no one in the room is going to tell the class bully not to pick on the class victim. Yet we all wish he would stop. What we can do is refuse to laugh, or look away, or anything else that will make the bully feel self-conscious or less comfortable. We know how we feel when we tell that hysterically funny joke and no one even smiles. We want to crawl away and shrivel up. This is the same feeling the bully experiences when he is not encouraged by others.

In the beginning, you—as the teacher—may have to point out someone who is being unkind and getting support from his classmates and show how they are giving tacit approval. Someone eventually says "Stop giving tacit approval" to someone putting down another classmate. I have been doing this for years, and I have seen class after class catch on and become empowered.

I once had a new girl come into my class after having been expelled from another school for hitting a teacher. She sauntered into my room, and when I told her she would need a notebook, she said, "I'll get one if I feel like it, lady." She looked around, waiting for everyone to laugh because, after all, she had put down the teacher. She just got stares, and she fled the room. As I ran after her, I heard my kids saying, "It worked! We didn't give her tacit approval!" I had forgotten about the tacit approval strategy, but they hadn't, and suddenly they saw how they could make a difference. Indeed, they were empowered.

ONE IS A RAT—TEN IS POWER

I once had a student who was stealing schoolbags from other students, and I was sure that everyone but me knew who was doing it. I naively asked them to please tell me who it was.

Here I was asking some poor student to stand up and rat on the toughest bully in school. *Sure!* Finally, the bell went off in my head, and I realized I had asked the impossible. So I said to them, "I do not expect one of you to tell me because you don't want to be perceived as a 'rat.' I understand that. But I also know you all want this bullying to stop. If 10 of you tell me, you then have power. The thief cannot threaten everyone. So if you know who is doing it, please put a note in my mailbox with his or her name, and I promise no one will know you told me. However, if I don't get at least 10 of you to name the person, I cannot do anything about it. Empower yourselves and prevent yourself or someone else from being victimized."

The next day I had over 20 little scraps of paper from my newly empowered students. Being armed with this information allowed me to confront the student who was stealing and frightening all his classmates and to have him suspended. No more schoolbags were stolen, and the lesson about power in numbers was well learned.

Take note: Don't ask the kids to write down the name while the class is in session. They will hesitate when in the presence of anyone they fear.

The "Many Kids Told Me" Fib

This is the educational equivalent of the Witness Protection Program. We all understand that kids are afraid to tell on one another for fear of retaliation, fear of being ridiculed, or some such reason. Sometimes there is a student who is brave enough to tell you who has been beating up all the kindergarten kids and taking their milk money. At the same time, she makes you swear on your life that you will not say who told you.

So how do you confront the bully without evidence and without revealing your source? I tell the bully that *several* classmates told me what they saw, and with all those "witnesses," the bully usually breaks down and confesses. Actually, it is not a fib, just an exaggeration!

Don't Call Home

Don't call home? You are probably thinking, "This woman is telling us not to do what we were taught always to do." Let me clarify.

Unless we were born under a lucky star, we are bound to get our "worst nightmare" student in one of our classes at one time or another. We also know we are going to have to live with this nightmare for a whole school year. The last thing we want to do is alienate that student at the beginning of the term because, whether or not we want to believe it, some students can make our lives a living hell.

Many teachers believe in contacting the family right away to report any infractions. If you know there are cooperative parents at home, of course it may be a good idea. But what about those students whose parents will deal with your call in a manner that may make things worse? Or the parents who are ineffectual? Sometimes it's a good idea to "strike a deal" with the perpetrator. After having a one-to-one (see One-on-One on page 95), I inform the student that it is appropriate for me to call his parents. When the student grovels and pleads and explains how he will be grounded for seven years, I agree to *not* call if I have the student's word that he will at least make an effort to behave. (But don't make him promise to never misbehave. See Never Demand a Promise on page 104.)

Many times it really works because your students believe you are on their side. A point I must stress here: If it is something serious, you must inform the parents. If a child has missed 10 homework assignments, the parents need to know about it, whereas the two of you can probably negotiate about one or two missed assignments. But do not leave yourself open to a parent who says you didn't tell him his son was in danger of failing or his daughter was truant. That is serious stuff.

Softening the Call Home

Sometimes it is imperative that we speak to a parent. I believe students should make the calls home on occasion. When you reach the parent, you inform her that Steve will explain why this call is necessary. What you might consider is softening the call by telling the parent, "Steve wants to talk to you. He is having a bad day today." You and I might know that most days are bad days for Steve, but often parents don't want to hear that; so when you say that he is having a bad day today, you are softening it for everyone involved.

Tons of Quizzes

For some courses, I do not give big midterms and final exams. Instead, I give many small quizzes—let's say 15 during the term.

At the end, I tell them I will take the 12 highest grades and average them. It nullifies the few times a student may have been unprepared or just didn't do well. If a student misses three quizzes, however, there are no low scores to discount because I will count 12 grades.

This is a fair way of grading and rewarding good attendance, but it does involve a little more work for the teacher. I have found that some kids panic when everything hinges on one exam, and if I have only a couple of tests to go by, I really don't get an accurate overall picture of my students.

However, you would be remiss if you didn't assign the occasional heavily weighted project because the reality is that the real world has stressful tests like SATs and reading placement exams.

OFFER CHOICES

This Ginott (1998) strategy works extremely well with young children. (Ginott suggested offering choices to children so that they feel empowered.) If the class seems restless and you know they need a change, let them be the ones to decide what the change will be—sort of!

When you sense, for example, that they are growing tired of arithmetic problem solving, ask them if they would like to do something else. After that hurtful, resounding *"Yes!"* tell them they may choose either a spelling bee or a drawing lesson. What they do not have to know is that you were planning to teach these lessons all along. Giving them a choice makes them feel empowered. And you get to do what you had planned to do anyway.

CONFER FOR GRADES

At the end of each grading period, I have an individual conference with each student. It is usually done during an independent reading time. I first ask them to write down what grade they think they deserve and an explanation of what they did (or didn't do) to deserve it. Around 8 out of 10 students are usually right on target.

I think it is a wonderful opportunity on the students' part to try to convince you that they deserve a higher grade—and in some cases they do. How empowering to stand up for oneself! On the flip side, it is a lesson in humility for the truant who feels worthy of an A. It is a good opportunity to discuss frequent absences, missed assignments, and the effect behavior has on his overall performance.

Finally, there are those students who have a 90 average but will ask for an 80. Such students must be taught to believe themselves worthy. One of my favorite students, Liana, had a 96 average and asked for a 75. I asked her to please convince me why I should lower her grade. I believe modesty prevented her from asking for her rightful due, so I had to point out the potential consequences of her false modesty. (Oh, by the way, she got the A because she couldn't convince me she deserved a C.)

"CLASS"—THE COLLECTIVE NOUN

When a student is misbehaving, it is unfair to make the entire class stay after school. Yet sometimes a class has to work as one unit, as a *collective noun,* "a class."

I will often tell a class that they will go home as soon as everyone is quiet. If José feels like giggling, it is up to the class to let him know he is preventing the rest of them from going home. The class also has to learn to do this in a noncombative way—no "Shut up, stupid!" is allowed. Here is where the skill of not giving tacit approval comes in (see Tacit Approval on page 52). It's also your opportunity to give a quick grammar lesson on the definition of a collective noun.

INDEPENDENT READING, WITH TWINKIES!

Matias, a student teacher of mine, suggested that the whole class read independently at the same time. Because it was a particularly hard-to-handle class, I told him that I thought it would take them forever to settle down. But we managed to refine a strategy that would actually quiet them down somewhat painlessly.

We all went to the library and chose a book. I let them choose any fiction book they wanted to read that was within their reading-level range. They were told that if they were not enjoying the book, they had to put it back and choose something else. I did not want them to read anything they weren't enjoying because I wanted reading to be fun for them. I would let them sit anywhere in the room.

Many curled up in the doorway, some sat under desks, and some just moved into a quiet corner.

Now, what would make this reading lesson perfect? *Junk food!* So I would then bring out cookies and pass them out to the kids. Eventually, we had the cafeteria bring milk to drink with the cookies and other assorted gourmet snacks, such as Twinkies! (If you want to be a really nice person, you might give them a sugar-free snack, so those teachers who get them next period will not say terrible things about you! You might also see Sweets or No Sweets on page 64.)

Go With the Roll

You planned this wonderful lesson on the history of the Pony Express and you know it is going to wow them. But something happened along the way and suddenly the class is deeply involved in a discussion on the concentration camp at Treblinka. You have no idea how the discussion got *there,* but it is fascinating. The kids are sharing feelings, ideas, and incredible insights. Should you get them back on track? Not if you don't have to. You know they will be dealing with the Holocaust in the future, so stick with something that has magic today. Of course, you cannot always do that because of curriculum demands, so you have to use your judgment. Learning isn't always about lesson plans.

Incorporating Fads

I recently visited my nephews, Jack and Dan, and they were into the latest superhero. Their rooms were flooded with pictures, their vocabulary was superhero jargon, and needless to say, to be part of their world I had to pretend to be interested in their latest fad. No matter what age your students are, there is always some fad they are caught up in. A good teacher can incorporate the latest craze and the interest it generates into the lesson, making it educational and a lot of fun for kids.

Did They Learn What You Taught?

Sometimes I taught a lesson and assumed the students understood everything I taught. I just knew they would ace the test on the material they just learned, but to my dismay, I would be faced with many failing papers. Obviously, there was only one person who really understood the material, and that was me, but that didn't help the class. I had even asked if they understood and I should have taken the blank stares as the answer because we know kids are reluctant to admit they don't understand something.

A wonderful way to see if the class learned what you taught is to ask them to put their heads down and cover their eyes. Then instruct them to put thumbs up if they understood the lesson and thumbs down if they wanted further instruction. If most of the class understood, you would be able to privately help the few individuals who didn't grasp the lesson, and if most of the thumbs were down, I would try teaching it again, perhaps using a different teaching style.

ROLE REVERSAL OR ROLE-PLAYING

This is a wonderful strategy to make students look at themselves through your eyes, *and vice versa!*

When there is a problem in the class, try to role-play. Create a situation like the one you want explored, and ask for volunteers to be your cast of characters. You will learn that their insights usually help provide a refreshing, different perspective.

Let the kids know that you are stumped about how to handle a certain problem in the classroom. Ask someone to "be you," and you play the part of a student in the class.

You can use a role-play or a role reversal—either one is effective. The best part of this strategy is that it usually has a light-hearted quality to it and people laugh at what could otherwise be an unpleasant situation.

"AM I BORING?"

I did not use this tactic too often, but when you know your audience (see Chapter 13, Knowing Your Audience) this can be really fun and, more important, helpful to you as a teacher. This strategy stems back to a time when I was very insecure in a subject I was teaching. I was an English teacher at the time, but my principal threw in some history classes for me to teach. As a student, I had *hated* history with a passion because my history teachers seemed incredibly dry and boring. I suddenly had to teach about Ancient Greece, and all I knew about it was that it was old!

I crammed up on my history and was desperate to have my students enjoy the subject and not be "historically challenged" as I was. As I went along, I asked the class to let me know if I was losing them or turning them off. The best part is that I now love discussing Ancient Greece, and I like to think my students are discussing it as we speak.

Don't be afraid to ask the class if they are getting confused because it is better to know than to keep on repeating a sleep-inducing lesson.

CLASSROOM SUGGESTION BOX

This can be a great resource for teachers and for students. Having a suggestion box where your students can be anonymous (or not) can help you learn what your students want and can help your students express their needs. I have to warn you in advance that sometimes kids can be brutally honest and say what you don't want to hear, and sometimes they can be pranksters and suggest things like homework should be assigned once a year. You have to make it clear that suggestions are to be sincere and are a tool for you to make the classroom more conducive for learning. There were some years where I felt some of the suggestions made me a better teacher, and there were some years that it wasn't taken seriously and I removed the box.

A FUN WAY TO LIMIT SLANG

Many times, teachers try to talk like the kids so that there will be no doubt that their teacher is "cool." But more often than not, the teacher sounds ridiculous to the kids, as well as patronizing. No one is impressed by a 55-year-old teacher in orthopedic shoes who says, "Yo, dude, you ain't done no work." As a matter of fact, slang does not belong in the classroom. In the streets and in their homes, students are free to say whatever they choose, but in your room they should use Standard American English because the reality is that people often judge us by how we speak. I want my kids to sound as smart as I know they are! To do that they must first be aware that they are using slang or nonstandard English. Rather than correct them each time they use a slang word, I put the class in charge of eliminating the word. For example, if anyone says *ain't,* the class points and says, "Lowden will get you." The "ain't-sayer" has to smile and say, "Thank you." The kids really have fun with this because it is said good-naturedly.

We all had a good laugh when Stella was corrected. She indignantly looked at the class and said, "I ain't say *ain't.*" She had no choice but to laugh and realize that she had been totally unaware of her repeated use of the word.

A note here: Be careful not to devalue slang, which can be very colorful and cultural, but rather have your students learn how to differentiate and use language appropriately.

Don't Overcorrect

The previous strategy is one we don't want to abuse. If we keep correcting every grammatical error, then students learn to correct none. That is why I will just tackle one—for instance, "ain't" as I just described. Once they hear the error on their own, I'm on to a new one. "I seen" is a hot number in my school. Occasionally, I let an "ain't" slip in while I am speaking to see if my class is on its toes. They love saying, "Lowden will get you!" to Lowden herself (as I meekly mumble, "Thank you").

Student Revenge: Your Personal Evaluation

I call this "payback time." At the end of the year, I ask my students to evaluate the class they took with me—to tell me if they liked it and why, what I could have done to make it better, and what they liked best and least. It is up to you to include what you want to find out from them. They do not have to put their names on the papers, and I allow them the freedom to make comments. I stress that they should be as constructive as possible and should not be mean-spirited. (With a smile on my face, I do threaten to hire a handwriting analyst if anyone's comments are real mean!)

This is a good way for you to determine what has worked and what hasn't. My favorite response was from a student who wrote,

"I love your class because you are so funny—well, at least you try to be and we kids get a kick out of that!" *Try* to be?

"Help . . . I'm Being Observed!"

The moment you dread is getting closer. Your supervisor is going to come to your room armed with pen and paper to observe you. Please understand that your supervisor is not there to judge you, just to help you. (Say that over and over the night before because most of us don't sleep too well that night.) You're sure your lesson will fall flat while your students are running around the room acting out the definition of "riot."

Don't worry—that rarely happens. Some teachers explain to the students that there will be a visitor to watch *them*. I always told them that the visitor was there to watch how I teach and how we interact. I tell them that it is a very important time for me and that I am counting on them to help me. I am always amazed at how supportive the kids are.

One year, I explained to the class that their enthusiasm would be helpful, and I encouraged them not to sit there dumbstruck. I did an experiment in science, and what followed made me cringe with embarrassment. Each child passed my principal and said in a less-than-subtle, loud voice, "Wasn't that interesting?" or "Wow!" It looked totally staged, but fortunately he didn't see it, which to this day still amazes me. Knowing you have a class on your side makes the observation nearly painless.

I Bragged About You

This strategy is one I wish I had when I was worrying if my students were going to be stressed out during my observation as much as I was. As I mentioned, many teachers threaten their students and tell them that the principal is there to watch them and they BETTER BEHAVE. A wonderful idea is to tell your students how you brag about them and the principal is coming in to see the class in action. This way, they don't feel judged, they feel more relaxed, and best of all they have a reputation to live up to and they usually do.

CHAPTER TEN

Setting Consequences

EVERY ACT HAS A CONSEQUENCE

Now that the rules have been defined, it is a good idea to empower your students by having them help you determine penalties. One of my mantras is "Every act has a consequence." I cannot tell you how important it is to stress this, to convey the significance of individual responsibility.

Never give them ammunition to accuse you of being unfair. I always ask my students what they feel would be appropriate consequences in a given situation. Believe it or not, they are stricter than I would ever dream of being. Once, after a serious fight in which I was accidentally pushed, I asked the two participants what they believed would be a fair punishment. One boy suggested a month's detention, and the other offered to wash my car. Both punishments were inappropriate. A mere two days of detention was more than enough, as two days to them is an eternity.

Remember to stress that consequences can also be positive.

COUPONS, TICKETS, MARBLES, OR "MONEY"

Above are just some of the names for reward ideas, but they all serve the same purpose and that is to motivate students through positive reinforcement. The terminology you choose depends on the age of your students. You can reward them for individual accomplishments

and make the necessary corrections. They would then bring the corrected papers to my desk, where I would quickly go over them. If they overlooked a misspelled word, or if they didn't correct it properly, they got a "torture sheet"—a piece of scrap paper on which they would have to write the misspelled word 10 times. They'd moan and groan, and I would smile.

When a paper had no errors on it, I would feign disappointment. It is a lot of fun, and the "game" is to make Ms. Lowden sad by not letting her give them a torture sheet. Of course, the bottom line is that they are really careful to make sure they make no mistakes. This is also an excellent lesson in proofreading skills.

WHEN TO CALL HOME

As a teacher, my best suggestion is for you to call home when you think you should. Your gut feelings are usually what you should trust, as well as your philosophic beliefs. However, there are times you *must* call home. When a student is in danger of failing your class, when she is consistently not doing her work, when he is not showing up for class, when one's behavior is out of character, or if you fear a student is in any kind of danger, you must make that call. Often during adolescence, drugs and alcohol rear their ugly heads, and it is important for you to learn to see the signs.

AVOIDING CONFRONTATION

To have a safe and comfortable classroom, you have to do everything possible to avoid confrontations. Remember, other than their parents, your students probably consider you the most unfair person in the world. Kids have these universal characteristics where they will roll their eyes and suck their teeth while muttering, "It's not fair!" So the following strategies have been designed to make your room as "unfair-proof" as possible. If you apply these techniques, I guarantee that you will have minimal discipline problems.

I have watched teachers stumble because they would not or could not respect the needs of their students. Too often teachers feel they must exercise *control* over their students at the expense of genuine *communication.* Some of us go on automatic and say things we shouldn't. Try to raise your consciousness so you will stop yourself before there is a confrontation. Let's make that classroom safe and fun!

CHAPTER ELEVEN

Preventing Showdowns

GOING ON AUTOMATIC

Before I discuss strategies on how to avoid confrontation, let me try to assuage the guilt I am sure you will have for the times you "lose it." We all go on automatic occasionally. What I mean is that we yell, say things we should not say, and, in general, become the teacher we vowed we never would become. Come on, it will happen and it is okay *once in a while.* You are human and therefore have permission to err. The only request I have is for you to tell yourself you went on automatic and try to learn something from it. When I would go on automatic, I would say to myself, "Oh, well, I goofed." Realizing that is half the battle. Think of all those teachers who do the same thing and do not see the negative impact it has on their students.

And while we are talking about going on automatic, our students have to know that we too have our limits and have a right to our anger. A good suggestion is to confide in your class that you are feeling angry, tell them why, and tell them what *they* can do about the situation. If they want a fair classroom, they too have to contribute toward making it feel safe and not assume it is solely your job.

EVERYTHING IS EMBARRASSING

Having taught teens throughout most of my career, I know with some certainty that to them, everything is embarrassing. A new haircut that didn't come out like the picture in the magazine is sheer agony. A pimple is almost as bad as being told one has a terminal disease. Younger children often panic at the very idea of having to get up in front of a class to read. We all remember those moments. So be sensitive. Remember, embarrassing a student sets up a barrier between the two of you.

HUMOR, NOT SARCASM

Okay, I know a kid sometimes needs a real put-down, but as teachers, we should not be the ones to do that. Sarcasm is hurtful, and the less sophisticated student misses the sarcasm and takes it as a put-down (which it actually is).

I once witnessed a colleague of mine say to a student, "Maybe if you had half a brain you would understand." When the student responded with curse words, the teacher was outraged and called home. Later, when the teacher asked me if I had heard the boy curse at him, I asked him if he would ever speak to me that way if I wasn't paying attention to him. Of course he wouldn't. Then why did he think it was okay to talk to his student that way?

I want to impress upon you that a good laugh is a great tension reliever. It also connects us as human beings. However, sarcasm and humor at someone else's expense are totally unacceptable and can be downright cruel.

THE BIGGEST NO-NO: "ONLY KIDDING"

I would rather my students use swear words than hurt someone's feelings and then say, "I was only kidding." That is not allowed in my room. "Only kidding" is one of the few things that infuriates me, and my students know it. We talk about ruthless honesty—calling someone "fat cow" is not said to make someone aware that he has a weight problem, but rather to be cruel and insensitive. I tell them that if they want to make a joke about someone, try some self-deprecating humor. It can be very funny—after all, Joan Rivers made a fortune doing it.

"Shut Up—Not!"

I don't know if being told to shut up offends you as much as it does me. Try never to say "Shut up" to a student or a class. It's a demeaning and highly disrespectful expression. Asking someone to please be quiet or to calm down accomplishes the same thing without putting the student on the defensive.

"I Told You So"

Don't you just hate it when someone reminds you that he "told you so"? It seems we teachers can't wait to tell the student who we've reminded about something how we told them so.

"Didn't I tell you that you would lose your book?"

"Didn't I tell you that you would get into trouble hanging out with her?"

"I told you so. Now maybe you will listen to me."

Sound familiar? Kids respond unpleasantly to that, and it usually gets their eyes rolling. If you do that and they react negatively, I will have to say "I told you so!"

Avoid Arguments

Here's a painful reality of the life of a teacher: When you get into an argument with a student (other than one that's academic in nature, of course), *you* usually lose, even though it may appear that you won. When bickering with students, we lose some of our dignity in front of the class and find ourselves in the middle of a power struggle.

If the verbal haranguing goes on for more than a minute, I suggest you call a truce and have a one-on-one after class.

Globalizing

"You never do any work" and "you always wait for the last minute" are common chants when we go on automatic, but they accomplish nothing. All the teacher is doing is flinging an unprovable accusation and drawing attention away from the current issue. To avoid a confrontation, zoom in on the specific problem at hand. Be clear and precise without making any insults that are provocative.

Choose Your Battles

Sometimes we just have to overlook a minor broken rule, and I stress *minor*. If you are a teacher who yells constantly about every major and minor infraction, your students stop hearing you after a while. In my classes, I did not yell often, but rather I used the hard stare, the smile, the "Excuse me," the lowering of my voice, and the other strategies mentioned earlier in the book (see, also, Chapter 12). When nothing else worked, I found myself losing it (see Going on Automatic on page 67) and would become the irate teacher I had hated in the fifth grade. My kids would sit up, and I'd hear them whisper, "She really means it." Because I treated minor infractions lightly, my students took the rare display of anger quite seriously.

Don't forget, you can win the battle but lose the war. One of my students stopped coming to school because he was constantly being punished by most of his teachers for minor things, which I truly believed he could not help. So what was the result? He just stopped working.

Start All Over

Sometimes situations get so out of hand that there is irreparable damage. A student has said horrible things to you, and you don't think you will ever forgive her. You have violated every standard you set for yourself the day you became a teacher by trying to hurt her back.

After you cool off, you owe it to both of you to start all over. You might speak to the student after school, agree to a cease-fire, and go on as though nothing has happened. Don't rehash the incident that brought you to this point because nothing will be accomplished and the hurt will only intensify. There is usually a little awkwardness for a day or two, but after that there is something of a secret bond there as well.

Beware of Empty Threats

We all know the teacher who screams, "I'm going to have you suspended" and "I'm going to call home" and so on. Then he cools down and does nothing. It may work once, but after a few times your students will catch on and you will lose your credibility. (If you follow the next strategy your credibility rating will soar.)

No Spur-of-the-Moment Rules

Very often, a teacher will condemn behavior that was never defined as wrong, and, as a matter of fact, was usually tolerated. To a student, it feels as if you just made up the rule, and in some cases that may be just what you did. This is really unfair, and if you are called on it, you should let that particular infraction slide this one time but define it clearly to prevent it from happening again. A teacher with whom I once worked used to let the boys wear hats in the room (even though it was a school infraction). One day, a boy disrespected him, and he got the boy in trouble for wearing a hat. Now that's unfair!

Set Up Winning Situations

There are victories in losing battles. This strategy can have a wonderfully positive effect on a class or on a student. One day, my daughter came home from school very energized. It was a new term, and she had asked the teacher to consider a clean slate for grades rather than the traditional cumulative approach, which would reflect grades from the beginning of the year. The teacher said, "I don't like your idea. Tell me why I should do what you suggest." Felicia, who was not usually outspoken, got into a lengthy debate with her and "convinced" her. The class cheered, and my daughter was the hero.

When I met with the teacher, I asked her if she had set up the situation. She winked and I knew. She said, "I hope Felicia has the confidence to always speak up for what she believes." She definitely made an impact on my daughter!

PLAGIARISM

I have mentioned the advances of the Internet and one such advance should serve as a warning to your students. Many schools have programs that can search out a line from a paper and bring up a plagiarized term paper. Kids can get information that used to take days of research in a matter of seconds. They can also get book reports written by others and pass them off as their own. To avoid confrontation, make it very clear that you check for plagiarism. This might prevent some students from taking the easy way out.

Years ago a student proudly handed in a book report. I knew he hadn't read the book and I told him so. He was indignant and swore on everything sacred, until I pointed out that the main character, whose death he described so vividly, died only in the movie version! So you might also warn them that movies based on books are often very different from the books.

DON'T FORCE STUDENTS TO LIE

In my parent workshops, I hear parents force their children to lie and then accuse them of being liars.

For instance, a father gets a call from school about his son's truancy. The boy walks in and the father asks how school was. The son says, "Fine." The father is outraged at his lying son. The child lied to get out of deep trouble with his dad, but it was the father who was dishonest first. If he had been honest, he would have told his child about the phone call, but he chose to trap his son in a lie.

So when you, the teacher, see a student where she shouldn't be, be up-front right away. Don't expect a student not to lie when forced into a corner. Haven't you ever complimented a woman on her hideous dress when asked if you liked it?

MAKE RULES SPECIFIC: NARROW THEM DOWN

One of my pet peeves is when a school sets rules such as "Hitting a teacher is forbidden." To me that is a given. Is there one student who really thinks it is okay to raise a hand to a teacher? So why all the rules? But it does sound good to the parents and to the rule makers if there are lots of rules.

The reality is that students seldom read the rules if there are too many. I like to eliminate rules that everyone knows are infractions and clarify those that are questionable. For instance, my school has a rule that says, "Every student is to dress appropriately for learning." What does that mean? Every child should wear a "thinking cap"? It needs to be spelled out. Perhaps it means no hats, no tank tops, no miniskirts. Only then will it be clear—and rules that are clear and specific will attract readers. We mustn't write rules that look like the standard contract we are asked to sign when we buy a new car.

No Sides

Two against one is never fair. Even if you agree with one student, as a teacher it is up to you to mediate a situation, not decide who is right. Of course, good judgment is required here. If one student is being abusive or threatening, you must intercede. But most arguments can be worked out, and often if you take sides, you end up being the bad one. I did it once, and with all my good intentions, ended up being accused of trying to break up a good friendship.

Time-Out

I talked about avoiding arguments, and again I stress how important that is. Sometimes, after you have tried every trick in the book, you may have to give a child (it is easier with younger students) a time-out. You might excuse her from continuing a lesson and allow her to put her head down on the desk until she is able to work. You might suggest she sit right outside the door until she cools off. Try and suggest this with compassion and not with anger. Sometimes we have to hone those acting skills that we, as teachers, all have.

No Comparisons

Do any of you recall the time your parent compared you to your brother or sister? Or asked why you couldn't be like little Nancy, the girl next door who seemed to do everything right? We all heard that and hated it, so let's not do it to our students. I remember telling one class how much more work I was able to accomplish with another class, and one girl put me in my place. She came up to me after class and said, "We are not the other class, and it hurts my feelings when you compare us. You remind me of my mother." Ouch! I felt terrible and vowed never to do that again.

I had one teacher friend who, although well meaning, told each class it was her favorite. When students compared notes (and they will!), they discovered what she had done, which totally devalued her compliment.

Each class is an individual group with its own dynamics. Teaching would be boring if all classes were the same.

NEVER ATTACK PERSONALLY

A student's character should never be criticized, but rather it is the act you disapprove of. No teacher should ever tell children they are hopeless or bad or lazy. Rather than attacking their character, explain what they are doing that upsets you.

For example, if you catch a girl cheating on a test and she denies it, don't call her a liar and a cheater—rather, tell her that you are disappointed because she copied word-for-word from the book and didn't tell you the truth.

DISTRACTIONS

When you sense there is student restlessness due to a pending fight, anxiety about a party after school, or even boredom, you need to distract them. I am not telling you to run around with a lamp shade on your head, but I am suggesting that you have an alternative to whatever you are doing. I always had a word search or some kind of math puzzle on hand. If there is a fight brewing, engage the potential "sparrers" with some kind of dialogue. You can also try turning off the lights to get their attention.

Chapter Twelve

Alternatives to Yelling

The "Teacher" Look

Yelling should be avoided at all costs because if you scream all the time, trust me, you will soon not be heard. There are a few simple strategies that might deter you from committing verbal violence (and prevent you from getting a serious case of laryngitis). One is the infamous stare. Locking eyes with a student who is distracting you or the class often gets him to refrain immediately. Once it is obvious that the student has picked up your signal, you can even offer a wink. It shows that you are not angry anymore and that you appreciate his display of respect.

The "Excuse Me" Smile

Another technique is one we all heard from our own teachers. You know, where you just stop what you are doing and say in the sternest voice you can muster, "*Excuse me,* but *I* am talking." There will always be that student who responds, "You're excused," in which case I suggest you first try a smile and go on.

The smile, by the way, should be a common expression on your face. A warm smile means a warm teacher—or so they think. I am not giving you permission to grin all day because you may then come off as *weird,* but a sour face is never fun to be around and is certainly not to be endured for a full school year.

The Lowered Voice

I have mentioned that you should not get into the habit of speaking over your students. The trick is to use a lowered voice.

When you are teaching, you may hear just a slight buzz in the classroom, and your tendency will be to raise your voice just a bit. But soon you'll hear just a little more talking and you'll raise your voice just a little more. When you finally hear the roar of the class and the shriek coming out of your throat, you'll know you put this strategy into practice too late.

So speak a little softer as soon as you hear that initial buzz. When people are straining to hear, they stop talking and often tell the others around them to be quiet.

The Art of Gestures

Another alternative to raising your voice is to gesture. There are many gestures that you should show your students within the first couple of weeks of the school year that will save your body and soul wear and tear. Here are some examples: finger on your lips for silence, snapping fingers to attract attention or to hurry up a dawdler (beware that in some cultures this is considered rude—see Cultural Differences on page 88), thumbs-up for approval, and "tsk, tsk" for disapproval. My favorite is raising my hand and having the class automatically copy my movement by raising their hands. At the same time, they automatically get quiet and, for the life of me, I don't know why this works. I am beginning to believe there is a muscle that connects a slowly rising hand to a quieted mouth, although I have yet to prove this anatomically.

Clap, Clap

This works wonderfully with younger children when you want to get their attention to start a lesson. They think it is a game and it actually is, but the end result is a quiet classroom. What you do is have your class respond to your clapping by clapping the same number of times you do. If you clap once, they will clap once; if you clap three times, they will clap three times. (You can always call this a math lesson, but that is a stretch.) What is really happening is they are listening to your clapping, and once they are listening, you can segue into your lesson.

HURRY, SHUT OFF THE LIGHTS!

No, I am not talking about a video I am about to show. I am talking about an instant attention getter. I usually use this strategy when I feel I am losing control of a class or when a fight is about to erupt. I turn off the lights, the class is momentarily stunned, and, for some reason, the class quiets down. Darkening the room is my equivalent of throwing cold water on someone—but not as messy!

PRAISING ONE

This works great with younger students. While they are getting settled you look around the room and say, "I see Lily is ready." Then you continue to look around and say, "I see that Paige and Dylan are ready to work," and suddenly you will see them all sitting eagerly waiting for approval. Kids love hearing their names called, so they may be quiet just to hear their names announced.

INITIALS ON BOARD

This has the similar effect as attention by praise, but it really gets them quiet quickly. With young kids, it is serious business; with older students, it's just kind of fun. When the class is unsettled, you put initials on the board of those who are ready to work. What happens is everyone looks around to figure out whose initials are up there. What they don't realize is that when they are looking to see who belongs to the initials they are looking with their eyes and the room gets quiet. I once got in trouble with my students when I put my own initials up there. They laughed and said I wasn't fair, so I had to convince them that I was part of the class too—I just happened to be the one with the chalk and the only one not talking.

VISUAL COMMANDS

As I have mentioned, many kids are visual learners, and for younger kids, holding up signs is very effective. When they are very young, holding up different colors gets an immediate reaction. When they see the color red, they know it means stop. You can have yellow signify they are to start getting ready, and then the green can be up while the class is working. Just think, you will have saved them a few pages from the Drivers Ed manual!

"I AM WAITING"

This is another visual technique that worked for me. One day I was doing all my tricks . . . the stare, the lowered voice, and just about everything else I could think of to settle the class down, but they just weren't cooperating. Just as I was about to screech and hate myself for it, I put the words "I AM WAITING" on the board and I sat down. For some reason, and I don't know exactly why, they settled down. I do have to warn you that you cannot do it too often because it will lose its effectiveness.

THE BELLHOP BELL

I loved my bell so much that I passed it on to my daughter. It is a bell just like the one you see on the desk of a hotel—you know, the one you ring to get attention. And that is exactly what I do!

I ask the kids not to move a muscle when they hear it. This becomes a game to them, and when they are still, I tell them how great they are and how much I love my bell. I then ask them in all seriousness to please be quiet when they hear the bell. As a reward, they will not have to endure my shrill shriek. (Beware: There is always one student who begs to ring the bell and goes on a power trip and can't stop!)

Someone suggested that a more pleasant sound is a rain stick. Although I like that sound, my classes probably wouldn't have heard it, but if yours would, it is a very comforting sound and can bring about the same result.

STOP TEACHING

You will have to decide for yourself if you want to try this strategy with chronically late students. I have no problem with it, but you might think it would embarrass the student . . . and you might be right.

Students arriving late to class can be disruptive and rude and ruin the tone of a class. Try stopping in midsentence while the latecomer meanders over to her seat. We all know what happens when the door opens after the class is in session. Everyone stops looking at the teacher, follows the late student with their eyes, and then finally the eyes go back to the teacher. So I join them. The reason this is effective is the very reason you may reject it: It may embarrass some students. All I can say is it does cut down on unexcused tardiness. I also knew my audience and I would use this technique only for students who were perpetually late and did not respect the rules.

THE TARDY QUIZ

A colleague of mine used to give an occasional "tardy quiz," a quick little test at the beginning of class. I would know she was giving it by the one or two kids camped outside her door after the late bell had rung. If students got to class late, the door would be locked and the latecomers got a zero on the quiz. Her students never knew when she was going to spring her quiz, and it sure got them to her class on time.

EARLY BIRD SPECIAL

If you are like me and find latecomers disruptive and annoying, you might use the positive reward method. I call it the early bird because you give the first five students who show up some reward. You can do this only occasionally, when they don't expect it, otherwise there would be too many students running wildly to get to your room. They also have to be coming from the same place, like from the cafeteria or the gymnasium. It wouldn't be fair if the student from the other end of the building had to compete with the student coming from the class next door.

An Imaginary Friend

This strategy can be used only with a class with which you have a good relationship and with one that knows you have a good sense of humor. When they are a little noisy and having trouble settling down, I kid around and pretend I am talking to a third person. This is really visual, so I hope you can see me talking to someone who isn't there saying, "I just don't understand these kids. Do you? How do I get them to be quiet?" Lo and behold, they usually chuckle and you again control the room. I still smile when I think of the boy who was laughing and said, "Oh no, Ms. Lowden is losing it." Again, you must know your audience and make sure they know you are kidding. The danger here is you can use this strategy only once; if used more, there may be rumors about your mental health.

Word of the Day

A fun way to teach a good vocabulary word AND a quick way to get a quiet classroom is to have a word of the day. Start by putting a word on the board and have them define it. Then you slip it into your lessons, and whenever you say the word, they have to respond to it. The ideal time to use it is when you are losing the attention of some students. Younger children can put their fingers over their lips or clap, and older children can raise their hands. The end result is both a quick way of getting a class quiet and a reinforcement of a new vocabulary word.

R-E-C-E-S-S

We all know that the favorite subject of the day for younger children is recess. Try putting the word R-E-C-E-S-S on the board in large letters. Explain that each letter represents a certain number of minutes when they can play outside or in the gym and have fun. If recess is 30 minutes, they know that if you erase one letter, they are losing five minutes of playtime. If they decide that they would rather play during a lesson instead of finishing their work, you let them know that they are wasting their recess time by the mere erasure of a letter. It is a good visual reminder and usually gets the work done.

CHAPTER THIRTEEN

Knowing Your Audience

GROUP DYNAMICS

Be very cautious about the dynamics of your group. You can give the same lesson to a different class with totally different results. The chemistry of the group can be determined only after a couple of weeks. I did successful cooperative learning in groups of five with one class, but the same lesson bombed in another because I didn't realize that members of the second group were at war with one another. Often you can tell a joke to a more sophisticated group, and you may get the expected chuckles. Other groups will hoot and get so carried away that you may actually think you have the potential to be a stand-up comic, when in reality they just wanted to be loud and obnoxious. (Yes, they can be obnoxious!)

DIVISION OF LABOR

A teacher always has one or two students who are her right hand (oops, I may get into trouble with left-handed people here). I always have some students who will yell at me for having a messy desk and then will proceed to organize it. But in all fairness, a classroom has to have an equal division of labor. I suggest you make a chart and have the class list as many chores as possible. Chores can range from running errands to emptying the pencil sharpener. I ask for volunteers and then I randomly pick students to fill unassigned tasks. Each month or so, the jobs are changed. Everyone must have a responsibility and it is up to you to see that no one is being exploited or underutilized. Don't always give girls the tidying jobs and boys the lifting jobs. Girls can take out the garbage and boys can straighten the room. It is a good idea to assign these chores so our students will get used to nongendered roles.

Don't Play "I Gotcha"

Ah, little Elena is talking and not paying attention. Now is your chance to call on her and ask for the answer to the question you know she didn't hear and show everyone in the room that talking does not pay. Good lesson for her? *No!* It is only going to humiliate her and that is spiteful on your part. You are also setting a bad example and damaging the safe environment that you have tried so hard to create. If she is really being disruptive, you may have to ask her to please pay attention, and, granted, that may be a little embarrassing, but it won't be humiliating. Being told to be quiet is never as painful as being perceived as dumb.

Deceiving Looks

As a teacher of prejudice awareness, I am well aware that we all form judgments about people merely by how they look. It may be certain clothing, a certain swagger, or certain mannerisms. I have had these huge guys and tough-looking girls enter my classroom in the most challenging manner. Was I intimidated? Absolutely! But please profit from my years of experience. Looks mean absolutely nothing. The toughest-looking child very often is the sweetest but covers it by walking like a thug, and the reverse is true also. You assume that the darling little guy with the horn-rims who sits right near your desk is going to be your pet, but often he chose that seat because it is easier to torment you from there. So do not form any permanent opinions based on how a child looks. Very often, the students are just trying to make a statement to their peers, which may be totally misread by you.

KIDS HAVE BAD DAYS, TOO

Read body language. Sometimes a student will come into the room and slouch in her seat. Her eyes may be downcast, and you just sense she is having a bad day. Chances are you are right. I usually will whisper to the student and ask her if she is okay. It's my way of saying, "I won't bother you." Many of my students lived in homeless shelters in New York, where I discovered that half the time they didn't get to sleep because of the conditions in which they were trying to survive. Hopefully, teachers will share that kind of information with one another, so these children can feel safe within the classroom. I have often let students sleep or even just tune out, but I would make them responsible for the work they missed. I've often had to stay after school with them to help them catch up.

NEGATIVE ATTENTION SEEKERS

Many years ago, my purse was missing. I was trying to remain calm as I skimmed the classroom aisle by aisle in search of a clue before I went into total panic. And there, to my shock and dismay, hanging out of Todd's desk, was the strap of my purse. He stole my purse and wasn't even smart enough to cover his crime—or was he? He was a very bright little boy, but because of this act he had to stay after school, his parents were called in, and he was the center of attention. I noticed he was almost enjoying it.

I have since had similar experiences, though not as extreme. After many years of teaching, it becomes obvious that some students will do anything for attention, even if it means getting into trouble. If you sense you have such a student, I suggest you get the child to the counselor, but when possible, find positive ways to satisfy the need for attention that he so craves.

GOOD KIDS CAN DO BAD THINGS

We have to be very careful not to call a child "bad." Unless you have a true sociopath in your class, you do not have a bad child; you have a child who may have done something bad. Focus on the behavior and not on the child. Tell the child that his actions were inappropriate, but never allow him to believe you think him a bad person. Good people make mistakes, and I hope that for every child who "messes up" there are people in the background stressing that he is really a good person—and I hope even more so that you are one of those people.

HOLD STUDENTS TO DIFFERENT STANDARDS

A principal of mine, Bea Ramirez, told me it was okay to hold different students to different standards.

A seriously disruptive child who had been kicked out of just about every class was contentedly sitting in the principal's office stuffing envelopes for a large mailing. I saw this as undermining the teachers by rewarding this student with a fun job. Ms. Ramirez pointed out that the child was sitting there quietly doing "work," and that if a child had broken a leg and could not partake in sports, she would likewise be sitting there stuffing envelopes.

This disruptive child suffered from an impairment. She could not control herself in class if her life depended on it. Ms. Ramirez let the student work with her and then sent her back to class in a more relaxed mood.

The lesson? We seem to show much more compassion for students who have physical disabilities than those with emotional ones. Think about it.

IF YOU DON'T TRY, YOU CAN'T FAIL

If a child is failing in your class, don't just accept it—explore the possible causes. Perhaps the work is too difficult, perhaps the child has poor work habits and opts not to do any work, or perhaps computer games and TV have taken priority over books.

I have discovered another common pattern for you to store in your mind somewhere. Have you ever been afraid to take a test, and as a result, you didn't study and failed? I have had students who became petrified before an exam and froze. A student doesn't study so that when she fails, she can rationalize that it was because she didn't open her books—not because she is dumb! You can't lose a race if you don't run, and you can't feel like a failure if you don't study. So the failure is face saving because it has a logical rationale.

Find out from parents if their children are studying at home. Parents should be aware of this problem and can help them study until their confidence is restored.

Too Much Push on Sports

Sports are important for body and mind, and I am never going to say we shouldn't encourage them. However, there is often too much stress on sports. Boys (more so than girls) are usually made to feel like there is something wrong with them if they do not show an interest in sports or are not good athletes. We have to let boys know that sports are not the end-all and that there are many other areas in which they have a chance to excel. Conversely, we should encourage girls to take an active role in sports if they show an interest.

"Can We Really Be Anything We Want?"

Too often, a teacher will make a blanket statement to a group of students, telling them that they can be anything they dream of if they really try. What about those students who try and try but, sadly, do not have the ability to reach their goals? The severely learning-disabled girl who wants to be a doctor or the mediocre athlete who wants to be a shortstop for the Mets might need a reality check. As a teacher, I think it is irresponsible to give students false expectations when one knows they are not realistic. I don't believe in brutal honesty either, so I try to channel their interests into more realistic goals.

It is important to stress here that we must always encourage them to hold on to their dreams. I just want them to know the importance of having a "Plan B" in case "Plan A" cannot be attained. Conversely, don't let the underachievers who score off the charts in every standardized test beat themselves up into believing they are failures. They too need a reality check to unleash whatever is holding them back.

Audio or Visual?

A friend of mine read me the description of the course she was taking at the local college. After reading it to me, she asked what

I thought of it. I had to take the paper and read it to myself before I could give her my opinion. You see, I am a visual learner and so are many of your students. There are others who have difficulty reading concepts, yet grasp them immediately when they are orally explained. It is helpful for you to recognize these tendencies in your students.

A good idea is to have the class read some passages silently first and then ask for volunteers to read aloud. Often when students read aloud before reading silently, they have no idea what they have just read.

CHECK THE SENSES

When a child is having difficulty reading, please consider that she may have a visual problem before you write her off as having a learning disability. If a student keeps asking you to repeat something, don't assume he is stalling for time—he may not be hearing well. Notice where all your students hold their books to see if they are having a problem reading the print. You would be surprised at how many kids slip through the cracks when their visual or aural impairments are overlooked. I hope you will be observant and note those students and see to it that they get the glasses or hearing devices that they need. . . . Getting the students to wear them is often the greater challenge.

RESPECT PRIVACY

Very often, you want to know something that a student will not share with you. I have heard teachers cajoling students into telling them things about which they had no business asking, though most times with the best of intentions. Many times, you feel there is something your student is withholding from you, and you may be right. However, if your student is telling you there is nothing wrong or doesn't want to talk about it, you have to leave it at that. Privacy must be respected. After assuring the student that you will always be there if she needs you, you must back off.

A Secret Is a Secret, Unless . . .

Sometime during your career, a student may confide in you and ask you to promise you will not tell anyone what he has told you. Never make that promise—you may not be able to keep it. Remember, you are neither therapist nor doctor and can be held responsible for withholding information that can prove detrimental to a student's physical or mental health. I have had students share their feelings of suicide, physical and sexual abuse, drug use (either personal or familial), and unwanted pregnancies. Many secrets can remain between the two of you, but none of those just mentioned should. You will have to be honest with your student and explain that you must tell the authorities. I have had students feel betrayed by me, and let me tell you, it is an awful feeling. At the time, they experience only the betrayal and not the rescue.

Not too many years ago, a student who was a victim of abuse would not speak to me because I reported her case. I saw her two years later and was surprised when she gave me a bear hug that knocked the wind out of me. She had blossomed into a self-assured young woman. And guess what? She credited me for that. Of course, it is the foster mother with whom she eventually lived who deserved all the credit.

Ignore Reputation

Inevitably, teachers will offer you their condolences when they hear you have certain students in your class. These students' reputations precede them, and as you wait for them to enter the room to wreak havoc, you find yourself discovering the power of prayer. Many times they live up to your expectations, but most times, if you can erase what you heard from your mind, they are a piece of cake with you.

As teachers, we do not treat all our students the same. We enjoy some more than others, and perhaps—though we shouldn't—we get annoyed with others too quickly. Well, that goes the other way, too. Your students do not treat all their teachers the same, and you may be the one teacher they like and respect. Don't set yourself up for a self-fulfilling prophecy.

PERMISSIVE VERSUS OVERLY PERMISSIVE

Permissiveness is an attitude of accepting the childishness of children. Knowing that a young child can sit only for a certain period of time shows you respect the age of your student. Six-year-old children may roll on the floor laughing at the mere mention of the word "poop." So what? They are only six. Teenagers will laugh at anything dealing with their puberty. So what? They're teenagers.

Being overly permissive is another matter. Overpermissive behavior allows undesirable acts that bring about increasing demands and encourage negative behavior. If you allow students to stroll into your room at their leisure, don't be surprised if as the term progresses, they walk in as the dismissal bell rings. Not setting limits brings about these negative behaviors. It is up to you to know the difference between being permissive and overly permissive, and to point it out to your students.

CULTURAL DIFFERENCES

When I began teaching, a little boy was acting rude and I was giving him a stern lecture. He wouldn't look me in the eye, and it infuriated me. I don't remember which Central American country he was from, but he had been taught there that it was disrespectful to look a teacher in the eye—respect was shown by looking down. In a similar vein, one of my Asian students told me it was considered improper to challenge the teacher.

Acknowledging, accepting, and appreciating cultural differences can prevent serious misunderstandings. You might suggest to your principal that it would be a good topic for a faculty conference, especially if you are in a multicultural school. If you have a culturally diverse class, seize the opportunity to have your students share cultural differences unique to their particular group.

A friend of mine suggests that teachers who have multilingual classes learn some common phrases in the native tongues of their students. It puts the students at ease and allows them to chuckle when you mispronounce a word or phrase in their language. (Don't be offended if they laugh at you; it is really making them feel confident because they know something you don't.)

What Language Is Spoken at Home?

In our multicultural society, we are finding more and more of our students are first generation in this country. It is a good idea to ask in the beginning of the year what language is spoken at home. Sometimes we speak to a parent and find they do not understand what we are telling them. If you know this is a potential problem, you might find someone (and often you don't want it to be your student) to interpret. It is the teacher who goes the extra five yards, who learns a few words in the parents' native tongue, that makes the parent comfortable and less self-conscious. The parents will usually have a warm smile on their faces because you are trying to speak their language, and it might encourage them to try to speak English.

Quality, Not Quantity

You have a student who hands in a neatly written 12-page paper, although you asked for a 1-page essay. Don't you feel awful when after you read it, you don't like it? Many children feel they will get more approval if they hand in *a lot*. You have to stress that quality is more important than quantity. I always chuckle when I assign a 150-word paper and I see the little numbers in the margin where the student counted the number of words. I smile because I remember doing it, believing that my teacher would count every word. I guess kids don't change—they still think we don't have a life! Of course these days, it pertains only to in-class essays because computers have the word-count feature.

Confusing Neatness With Responsibility

When a student hands in a neatly printed assignment, we often think a lot of effort went into it. In many cases it did, but that should not be an assumption. Conversely, penmanship that looks like that of a chimp should not be devalued. Difficult-to-read penmanship is often something a student can't correct. Although I do encourage all of my students to work on their penmanship, I also encourage those with really poor penmanship to use a word processor if they have access to one, so they won't get discouraged and my life will be easier.

Describe a Fight to a Potential Pugilist

In my school, physical violence was much too commonplace. There was a hardly a day that went by when there wasn't a fight. I used to think that these children just wanted to fight to show how tough they were. But after a few years I realized that in most cases it was not the two fighters who wanted to engage in battle, but rather the other children who wanted to stand on the sidelines where it was safe. I have seen children push two other students into one another hoping to get a good fight going. I have heard instigating that would prompt *me* to put up *my* dukes. Kids will use any strategy to goad the fighters to punch it out.

What I do is gather the two potential fighters and point out how everyone wants to see their blood, and how their "friends" will not let up until one of them is hurt. (I am usually quite graphic here.) In 9 out of 10 cases, it is apparent that neither one wants to fight, so I give them an out by blaming the spectators. They walk away relieved that they were given an out.

The Sound-Off Minute

This strategy works only once because it is a quick-fix solution that is not meant to remedy deep, recurring problems. But take it for what it's worth and use it with discretion.

When I have a student alone in my room who is really upset with me, I offer every student's dream—that is, the opportunity to say anything to me that she wants, with a promise that I will not in any way punish her afterwards. The only drawback is that she has exactly 60 seconds to sound off and get it off her chest. The initial reaction is, "Huh? I can say anything?" I explain that it is an uninterrupted minute, free of reprisal. What usually happens is a student will gripe and whine and tell you that you are the worst teacher on the entire planet and so on. When you say, "Okay, the minute is up," there is usually a giggle and most of the anger is dissipated.

PART IV

Showing You're on the Same Team

In this section, I have included my favorite strategies for creating a comfortable classroom and for reinforcing the concept that you and your students are on the same side. For a classroom to be comfortable, we must all feel safe. Our students have to deal with teachers, parents, and other students; they have to go out into the world and meet challenges. As a teacher, I give them "Lowden's Life Lessons," which I will explain in more depth later in this chapter. Basically, they are suggestions to help get through life a little more easily. Whether or not they choose to follow them is completely up to the students.

In my classes, we share so much. Students are so open—not because I am so wonderful, but because I am not their parent! I do not judge them, and I don't have the power to cut off their allowances or telephone privileges. I am safe for them, and you should be too!

CHAPTER FOURTEEN

Communicating Like a Pro

ACKNOWLEDGE FEELINGS

Very often students, especially teenagers, will come to you with what feels to them like an earth-shattering problem. Many times the problems are serious, but most times they are really, in the whole scheme of things, not that terrible. Listen to them and acknowledge their feelings, but don't tell them they are silly to worry or that their "crisis" is not important. When I hear a student sobbing after a boy breaks up with her, I know her heart is breaking. She really believes it when she says she will never love anyone again and is going to run off to join a convent. It's easy to tell her there will be many more boyfriends and that this is just "puppy love." To this teen, her agony is *real,* and trivializing the situation is exactly what she does not want. Acknowledge her feelings and tell her that even though you know it is painful, you also know that she will survive, and that you'll be there if she needs to talk to you.

NEVER DENY PERCEPTION

I remember a student complaining that her teacher picked on her and no one else. My knee-jerk response was to say, "Right, Casey, only you!" But that would serve only to alienate her more and to put her on the defensive. So instead I said, "It must feel terrible to feel your teacher picks on you. Why do you think she does that?" She then believed I understood, and she was able to carry on a dialogue with me in which I could offer a bigger perspective.

I've said this before, but I will remind you again that our perception is our reality. Did you ever feel unloved by someone and they just laughed at you for being so silly? One doesn't need laughter, but rather someone to acknowledge what you are feeling and then be reassuring.

Use "I" Messages

I have been trained in conflict resolution, and one of the best strategies it uses is the "I" message. Basically, this means communicating your wants, needs, and concerns without attacking your student. Instead of saying, "You don't do a bit of work here, and you're going to flunk," you might say, "I feel you're getting behind in your work, and I'm concerned that I will not be able to pass you." I have even gone so far as to tell a student that I felt she disliked being in my class and asked if there was anything I could do to make our year together more enjoyable. Her behavior changed after that, and to this day we keep in touch. I truly believe she didn't realize I had feelings and could be hurt. A high dose of honesty is strong cement.

"Let's" Instead of "You"

I can't stand it when I visit my doctor and she says, "How are *we* today?" Likewise, I'm annoyed by the waiter who asks me, "Hi, what are *we* going to have to eat today?" But in the classroom, it is nice to include yourself as part of the group. It really supports the "same team" concept. "Let's take out our books" is nicer than "Take out your books." "What can *we* add to the story?" is more comfortable than "What can *you* add?"

Interchange Gender Pronouns

I grew up thinking everyone was male unless otherwise stated. My teachers referred to everyone as *he* (except ballet dancers, nurses, secretaries, and "lady" doctors). The English language should be inclusive because young girls and boys do not understand generic language. They take everything literally and internalize what they hear. So the boy who never hears a nurse referred to as *he* or the girl who never hears a scientist referred to as *she* is hearing gender roles being assigned by us when we should not be doing that.

One year, a seventh grader confessed that as a little boy he always thought girls were lucky because they didn't have to worry about getting eaten by "man"-eating sharks. It was a wonderful example of how young children are so literal.

You will notice throughout this book that I alternate masculine and feminine pronouns. You may also be aware that when "she" is used, it is more conspicuous. Hopefully, one day we will no longer notice.

Limit the "You Shoulds"

Recently when my daughter visited, I told her she should cut her hair, she should do a certain lesson with her class, she should . . . she should . . . she should. In her most tactful way, she suggested I try not using the phrase *you should* so much. She said that is something she became aware of when she began teaching. Rather than telling a student he should write something this way, my daughter would say, "Have you thought about writing it another way?" or "You might try it this way." This strategy empowers the student.

(By the way, I asked my daughter if she had "considered" a shorter hairstyle. It's *still* long. So much for that strategy!)

One-on-One

Embarrassing a student of any age by yelling at him can be pure agony. Asking a student to speak with you after class or after school, one-on-one, can result in miracles. The student has no audience to entertain, and you don't have to show how tough you are in front of an entire class. You can engage your students in conversation about things unrelated to school and air your grievance at the same time. You might also ask your student why she thinks you want to speak with her. It gives some good insights.

On occasion, I have even called a student at home. Very often, speaking on the telephone—an inanimate object—is a benign way to discuss the problem the two of you are having. Sometimes it works really well. Other times the phone lines scream with pregnant pauses. Prepare what you are going to say on the phone, but don't overprepare because you have to listen and respond to what your student is saying. Your conversation depends as much upon your student's responses as on what you planned to say. Make sure you "know your audience" before you make the call. Your goal is to make sure there are no hard feelings.

HOW TO LISTEN

Haven't we all seen a teacher holding a student captive with fingers waving in the air and a nonstop barrage of reprimands? With that we hear a meek little "But, but, but. . . ." from the poor student who cannot get a word in edgewise.

I am sure we all agree that in all fairness we ought to listen to our students. I am not saying to give them equal time—even though I should—but at least give their point of view some respectful consideration. Here are a few strategies on how to listen.

While a student is talking to you, be conscious of your body language. You should be looking at him—not straightening your desk. A few "Uh-huhs" and a nodding head always help one feel that you are listening. In addition, you might pose a question about what he said.

Occasionally, a student would come to me with a pressing problem, and I would ask him to pull up a chair and sit next to or opposite me, preferably at a student's desk. Sitting at either side of the teacher's desk or standing while your student is seated is not conducive to comfortable communication.

MAKE LIMITS TOTAL RATHER THAN PARTIAL

We have to be careful with limits. Remember the old adage, "Give 'em an inch and they'll take a mile"? There is a certain amount of truth to that. If your rule is that there will be no unexcused lateness without a consequence, then that is the rule. Don't allow them to wander in three or four minutes late after you've already set a rule.

I did not allow gum chewing. I would always get a request to allow gum chewing with the stipulation that if someone makes gum-chewing noises, then everyone has to spit it out. I once allowed myself to get talked into that. What a nightmare that became! I heard bubbles being popped, and when I said, "Okay, no more gum," there was a chorus of protests with everyone pleading for one more chance. I learned my lesson because had I made the rule firm, I would not have had the confrontation at all. Remember, our goal is to avoid confrontation, and we do that by making ourselves clear.

My rule is not a partial rule, it is *the rule.*

STATE RULES IMPERSONALLY

By stating rules impersonally, you are focusing on the rule and not on the child. I get upset when I hear teachers say things like, "What's wrong with you? Can't you follow the rules?" How can we expect someone not to react defensively?

However, it is totally nonconfrontational when we just remind a child who is wearing a hat in your class that the rule is "No hats allowed." Period! End of argument! (Even better—no argument!)

VAGUE ALLEGATIONS

Nothing is more confusing and more confrontational than vague and/or unclear statements. Too often we go on automatic and say things like, "Act your age," "Stop acting silly," and so on. Those comments are sure to get an indignant reply, so we have to be specific. Acting your age doesn't mean anything to a 9-year-old (or for that matter to a 90-year-old), so point out exactly what you mean. "I want you to stop talking to Phoebe and to read quietly." By being clear and specific about what you want, you are more likely to get it.

DESCRIBE WHAT YOU SEE (OR DON'T SEE)

To avoid confrontation, we know not to call our students *lazy, careless,* or *bad.* What we do instead is describe what we see without passing judgment. "Fern, I see only one page done when there were supposed to be three." Or, "Allen, I don't see the assignment you were supposed to complete." Calling students names will only elicit a defensive reaction. Merely state what you see and avoid confrontation.

PICK A RULE AND STICK TO IT

This is an invaluable strategy that has to do with perception. Too many times we resort to nasty, empty threats. I must admit that I am not guiltless here, but I've discovered a wonderful way to alter perception.

In order to set a standard, I choose the rule I hold most sacred—the one concerning unexcused lateness, which I find intolerable—and always enforce it. Latecomers distract the class and show a disregard for all of us and toward the lesson in progress. I tell my students that I will gladly accept a late pass from a teacher, but if they choose to hang out instead of coming in on time, they will be penalized. I take off 1 point and there is nothing they can do to make up for the loss of this point. When we meet about their grades (see Confer for Grades on page 56), I then point out their tardiness, add up the minuses, and deduct them from the final grade.

I have had students who deserved a 70 for their grade, but had 15 points deducted for lateness. Needless to say, they failed and had no one to blame but themselves. Once they saw the tangible consequences of their lateness, I earned a reputation as one who means what she says. (You might have to stress a different rule if your school doesn't allow consequnces for lateness.)

Once when I was teaching my sex education class, for which they all knew they could not be late, the bell was just about to ring when I heard Michael yelling to his friends. "I can't be late," he exclaimed, "I have sex with Lowden now!" Thank goodness that comment wasn't taken out of context! We had a good laugh, but Michael was on time!

Some students will just cut and hope you think they are absent. Warn them that lateness results in only 1 point off, but that the penalty for cutting is just short of capital punishment. Here I must stress the importance of keeping good attendance records.

STAY SIMPLE: ONE WORD OR SENTENCE WILL DO

Oh, let's save us all some breath. Have you ever found yourself explaining in great detail why a student must do homework? It becomes one of those boring lectures we all hated when we got them from our parents and our teachers. Now we are doing the same thing. Catch yourself when you do that and just state what you want—period!

A colleague of mine had a party, and one of the girls left potato chips in her desk. He told her about the cockroaches the food would attract and what bad health habits she was developing and so on. She came to me and said, "I just wish he would've told me to throw away the potato chips—I would have done it in a second. I didn't even realize I had left them there."

The Desk Drummer

We all have had the students who drum on the desks with their fingers. You know what happens. You are teaching and suddenly you are almost dancing to the beat of your drummer and can no longer concentrate on your lesson. The reality is, most of them have no idea they are drumming and all you have to do is say, with a smile, "Lizzy, you are drumming," and she will stop. You can also clasp your hands together while looking at her without saying anything and she will clasp her hands together too. I have yet to meet a student who will not stop when asked that way. (However, I would be lying if I didn't say I had more than one who went back to an unconscious drum solo.)

Would You Talk to an Adult That Way?

I often hear teachers speaking to young people as though they were inferior beings. If you hear yourself criticizing a student, ask yourself if you would talk to an adult that way. Yes, I know they are not adults, but you would be a lot more sensitive to a peer. Why not be sensitive to your student?

Don't Futurize

When your third-grade pupil comes to school an hour late, don't remind him that he will never get a good job because he couldn't care less. Trust me, he's not looking for employment and so your forewarning means nothing.

When I teach my ninth-grade students about the horrendous consequences of AIDS, it isn't real to them because at 15 you don't believe you can die. However, when I graphically describe the physical effects of STDs, they swear off sex for life!

When I tell a fifth-grade student she will not get into college because of her bad study habits, she too couldn't care less. She is still anxious about middle school!!

So instead, make the consequences immediate. Make their future *tomorrow*. "If you enter my classroom late today, you will stay after school tomorrow." *That* is real to students.

PARAPHRASE

This is another popular strategy used in conflict resolution. Just paraphrase what you heard. When a student accuses you of being inhumanly unfair, repeat what you believe he said. You might say, "So you are saying that I am unfair because I expect too much from you?" The student is then hearing the words from you and can digest them more easily and address the issue. How many times have we said something that, when paraphrased back to us, sounds different?

DON'T MIX CRITICISM WITH PRAISE

I remember one night I made this delicious meal. My husband was effusive with praise, and I felt wonderful until he said, "If only you were neater in the kitchen." There went the compliment . . . I was a good cook, but a real slob.

In the classroom, we have to try to give unconditional compliments. Think about how often we say, "This is such good work; it just proves that if you stop fooling around, you can do so much." Wouldn't it be nicer to simply convey what great work the student has just produced? I am sure he knows all about his deficiencies, so why remind him in his moment of glory?

CURSING—YES OR NO?

As for cursing, I rarely allow it and only if it is appropriate. In my course on prejudice awareness, for example, if a student is sharing a personal experience and an inappropriate word slips out, I let it go so as not to kill the effect or the mood.

Of course, this is up to you. Students will often slip and apologize to me. I ask them to apologize to everyone. I want them to know that inappropriate cursing is an affront to everyone, not just the teacher. The same rule goes for burping. For some unknown reason, burping is hysterically funny to the "burper"—and usually to no one else.

FORCED APOLOGIES NOT ACCEPTED

Many teachers believe they are instilling responsibility in youngsters by forcing them to apologize to someone to whom they believe an apology is owed. How many times have I seen a teacher or administrator dragging bodily an unwilling "atoner"? "Barbara, say you're sorry to Ms. Lowden *now!*" Barbara looks at my shoes and mutters those assigned words.

Everyone is surprised when I do not accept the apology at that moment. I stop Barbara in midsentence and tell her she can apologize if she thinks she should—at a time when it is sincere. I have offered kids the opportunity to write about what happened, and if they think the situation was unfair, they can express it—or they can do nothing at all.

To me, a coerced apology has as much value as a coerced confession and often liberates the apologist from real consequences.

THE DOUBLE MESSAGE

I had no idea this was a strategy until my student teacher, Noam, told me how much he loved it.

One day, I was very angry at a girl, but while I was expressing my discontent, my hand was on her shoulder. I guess I was telling her verbally what angered me, as my hand on her shoulder was subconsciously telling her we were friends. If you are uncomfortable touching a student (see To Touch or Not to Touch on page 131), you can say something conciliatory that may make you both feel better. A gentle smile or wink can also alleviate a tense situation. Remember, a grudge helps no one.

WHAT WOULD ANOTHER TEACHER TELL ME?

Very often a student will come into the room accusing some teacher of being unfair, prejudiced, immoral, and sadistic. After talking to the student and using such strategies as paraphrasing and acknowledging feelings, you still have to calm this child down and find out if the allegations are exaggerated. (See Confronting Other Teachers on page 153.)

I remember Eric coming into my room accusing Ms. Sheff of hating boys. He told me that she always picked on boys and treated girls as if they were better. I then asked, "What would Ms. Sheff tell me if I asked her about this incident?" He proceeded to tell me she would complain that he never does his homework and throws things around the room. Got the picture?

CHAPTER FIFTEEN

Being Fair

ADMIT WHEN YOU ARE WRONG

Believe it or not, once in a while a teacher is wrong. Not me, of course, but others—yes.

Seriously, when you make a mistake, admit it. Too many people think it is a sign of weakness to make such an admission. To me, it is a sign not only of strength but of fairness.

I remember once pushing a very difficult student too far. I got him so angry he stormed out of the room and later opened the door and threatened me. The dean heard him and was going to suspend him. I asked if my student and I could talk privately. I admitted to him that I may have pushed too far, and he meekly said, "Maybe I over-reacted." I said I wouldn't call his home, but he had to assure me he would be indebted to me for the rest of his life, to which he eagerly agreed. (Humor lightens everything!) He became more responsible in my class, and I was one of the few teachers who had no subsequent confrontations with him.

ADMIT WHEN YOU DON'T KNOW SOMETHING

It took me many years to learn that many of my teachers did not know all the answers. They did what I call "the dirty trick," whereby a student asks a question to which the teacher does not know the answer, and the teacher says, "Good question. Why don't you research it and give us the answer?" Now, that is really dishonest!

Tell the children you do not know the answer, but you would appreciate it if someone would research it. If no one volunteers, you should research it yourself or assign it for extra credit. No one knows everything, not even teachers—even though we sometimes behave as though we do!

NEVER BREAK A PROMISE

The broken promise is similar to the empty threat. The difference is that the broken promise leads not only to a lack of credibility but also to disappointment. If you break a promise, then the "It's not fair" refrain is totally justified. Our students hold us to our word— as they should.

When you make a promise, cover all your bases. I remember promising a third-grade class a trip to the playground as a reward for a job well done. I did not check the weather report and offered no alternative plan in case of inclement weather. You guessed it: The day we were supposed to go to the playground was a nasty, rainy day. So as a rational human being, I promised them we could go the next day. In unbearable wailing unison, they explained to me, "But you promised. . . ."

You know, it's not that bad sitting on a swing in the park when it's raining!

NEVER DEMAND A PROMISE

Do you think you might be tempted to sell your soul in exchange for that winning $10 million lottery ticket? Well, asking a student to promise that he will never call out again in order to avoid detention is the equivalent of the lottery ticket. Remember, he may even mean it when he makes the promise, but we all know about good intentions.

Try simply asking your student to make an effort not to call out because making him swear on everything sacred usually doesn't work.

"I'M IN A BAD MOOD"

Whether you partied too much the night before, or your wife told you she's leaving, or you're just in a foul mood, you should warn your students. I have come to school with a very heavy heart and the last thing I felt like doing was teaching five classes, but part of the job description says I have to do just that.

One of the most difficult things is not to take your mood out on your students. So be fair and warn them. I have told my students I am in a sad mood and would appreciate it if they would help me by being cooperative. Kids are so amazing. They would usually jump on any student who misbehaved. (Be sure to let your kids know it's okay for them to ask for help if they're having a bad day too.)

I resisted the urge to tell them I was sad every day—think I would lose some credibility?

"THIS HURTS ME MORE THAN IT HURTS YOU"

Remember when your mom or dad said, "This hurts me more than it hurts you!" as you were being disciplined? I never really bought that line until I became a teacher. In dealing with misbehaving students, I have had to demonstrate consistency and firmness, and that has often entailed doing things I didn't want to do. Teachers must be skillful enough to convey that punishing *really* is not what we want to do.

I remember planning an exciting class trip to the zoo. It was going to be a reward for the class if they behaved in a manner we had all agreed to. But this particular group tormented every teacher who crossed its path, and I was faced with the question of how I could take them to the zoo. The problem was doubly challenging because I wanted to go to the zoo. I could have taken the easy way out and offered them one more chance, a "deal" whereby they could make up for their misbehavior and still go on the trip, and we would all be happy, especially *me*! But I couldn't do it because (a) they had not lived up to their part of the bargain, (b) they had betrayed my trust, and more important, (c) they had been disrespectful to other teachers and it would be a slap in the face to my colleagues if my class was rewarded for its poor behavior.

A few months later, after much improved behavior, we went to the zoo and it was truly a trip they had earned.

No "Boys Will Be Boys"

In my lessons on prejudice awareness, I talk about acknowledged and unacknowledged prejudice. We all acknowledge racism as a horrendous thing, as we should. We also spend money for programs to halt this bigotry, as we should. But we seldom get upset about sexism because we don't even realize we are perpetuating it. I have seen boys get away with things we would never tolerate in girls. How upset we get when a girl hands in sloppy work, even though many of us do not hold boys to that same standard. And when a girl curses, we automatically tell her she is not being ladylike, whereas we will tell a boy who curses he is not being gentlemanly only if there is a girl present. No one should curse—period!

In all fairness, we should not minimize the behavior of a girl who hits a boy. We should not give girls the domestic chores and boys the executive and physical ones. Boys and girls should be able to interchange roles to have more equal classrooms and a more equal society. (See also Interchange Gender Pronouns on page 94 and Division of Labor on page 81.)

Etiquette Pitfalls

Did you think for a second I was going to tell you to teach the boys the "ladies-first" rule? Not on your life! Before you start telling me about tradition, I am going to tell you we should treat all humans with kindness and respect. Good manners should be taught to all, and if they are gender based, they are sexist. Why can't a person hold the door for whomever follows?

Please and Thank You

I find that people don't say "please" and "thank you" enough, and, as a result, neither do our children. If you, the role model, use them often and encourage children to do the same, maybe we'll all get into the habit of being polite. I remember buying cookies and offering each student one as I walked around the room while they read. Not one student said thank you. I had to stop a wonderful silent reading period to point it out. They were sure they had thanked me, but no one had. The next time they nearly kissed me for the cookies. Making them aware was important because individuals often think they are very polite when in fact they may even be rude—and that applies to us, the teachers, as well.

GAUGE THE AMOUNT OF HOMEWORK

The teacher at the elementary level, or in the self-contained class-room, should be careful not to assign too much homework. Overload often leads students to accept the consequences rather than to do the work. Be fair, and you can even be kind by occasionally giving them the "night off."

In the secondary schools, where the subjects are departmental-ized, students often end up with five projects at the same time. Confer with your colleagues and impress upon your students that you need to be told when they are being overloaded with work. But beware the student who considers five math problems an overload!

CHAPTER SIXTEEN

Bonding Strategies

"I'M ON YOUR SIDE"

This is a strategy I picked up when my husband and then teenage daughter were having an argument. I think it was over something life-shattering, like the stereo was too loud.

With great exasperation, I heard him say, "Felicia, I'm on your side. I am your biggest fan." It really rang true because it *was* true. As a teacher, your students have to understand that you are on their side, and the best way to do that is to tell them.

After I assure them I am on their side, I explain why. "If you do well, I look good. If I have to fail you, I look bad!" In my course on prejudice, we learn that there is always an "us" and a "them." You have to establish that you are all on the same team and make it clear that you are an ally—not an adversary.

BEING VULNERABLE: SHARE A GIGGLE

Sometimes we think we have to be the stalwart teacher, never letting our guard down, never being vulnerable. Being human is a wonderful quality and we're even born with it. Every now and then let your students know you can take a joke and laugh at yourself.

Once I walked into my classroom and noticed an air of excitement that was almost out of control. I wanted to believe it was because they were about to learn how to parse a sentence, but just then

I noticed a whoopee cushion ready to be sat on by me! I had two choices: One was to get angry, and the other was to be the butt of their joke (pun intended). I chose the latter and made them suffer a bit before I plopped into my chair. It made the anticipated sound, and I just looked at them straight-faced and said, "Oh, my! Excuse me." They then knew I had seen it all along, and we all had a great laugh. Again, I knew my audience and was able to be part of a joke. Perhaps with a different group I'd have seen it as a mean-spirited act and would have had a different response.

Relating Your Own Experiences

Many teachers keep their private lives just that—*private*. It certainly is one's right. I, on the other hand, find that by telling my kids little anecdotes about my life away from school, I actually become human in their eyes. (But don't overdo it. You could become a bore and lose the focus of your lesson.)

I will never forget a first grader expressing shock that I had a family. Another student giggled at the thought of my having a first name. The funniest part of it was that he thought he was getting away with calling me by my first name when he would say, "Hi, Ms."—thinking Ms. was my first name. To many students, we are teachers and that is our life. Kids always say, "Get a life," and by sharing some of your stories from beyond the four walls of your school, they may actually believe you have one.

Staying Neutral

As teachers, and as human beings (we are both, though many of our students think they are mutually exclusive), we often have strong personal opinions. Having taught classes on prejudice awareness, I know how difficult it was for me to be neutral about my views on issues, but a teacher must. If a teacher is religious, she cannot impose her beliefs on her students. If a teacher believes that capitalism is an evil, it is inappropriate for him to share his personal political views. Be aware that if your students know you feel strongly about an issue, they may not want to share their own views in fear of it affecting their grade. They may also do the converse and say what they think you want to hear.

Our students are impressionable and we have to know when we are imposing our values on them. As our students get older, discussions about controversial topics are fine and indeed necessary. However, a good teacher allows all viewpoints and never states that one is better than the other, unless of course one is destructive.

THOSE SPECIAL FEW MINUTES

Be prepared, there are going to be some students who just rub you the wrong way. You just don't like them. They may whine, they may laugh too loudly, they may be show-offs, but in your heart of hearts, you feel shame for feeling the way you do. Don't! Your students certainly do not view all their teachers with equal admiration.

Even though it's natural and human to like some individuals more than others, one still has to refrain from playing favorites in any obvious way. The best way to make sure you don't show favoritism is to admit favoritism to yourself—and to no one else!

However, to ensure that I don't show favoritism, I occasionally put aside a couple of minutes to "kid around" with those difficult students or make them feel special in some way. I may include them in spelling sentences or send them on a special errand. This strategy assuages my conscience for not being perfect and not enjoying every student with equal intensity.

15 SECONDS OF FAME

I like to give as many students as possible their 15 seconds of fame. What I do is "personalize" my spelling sentences and my handouts by including my students' names.

An example would be:

Circle the nouns in the following sentence: "Shep and Annie think Ms. Lowden is the greatest teacher who ever lived."

You usually hear chuckling as they do their work. Just try to make sure everyone is included at some time and be careful not to be hurtful.

CREATIVE EXCUSES

You all know how we say, "The check is in the mail." What a boring and uncreative excuse for saying we forgot or that we're a little short this month.

Well, kids have *their* excuses, such as "I am late because the alarm clock didn't go off." The student knows (and I know) that she went back to sleep and pushed the snooze alarm 10 times too many. So I encourage my students to at least be creative and entertain me. I have had students attacked by a herd of wild bison while walking down Flatbush Avenue in Brooklyn, and I've heard about robbers who break into their homes late at night to steal the assignments they have so industriously worked to complete.

Have no fear, I still make them pay the consequences—only I do it laughing!

BEND THE RULES

Oh, come on, stop being a meanie! You know the rules and so do they. They know you don't let them walk around the room—but it is 95°F in the room, they are bored to death, and they can't bear to hear about one more Roman numeral. Today the no-walking rule seems impossible to uphold. So cut the lesson short and let them walk around a bit or chat with a neighbor. Bending the rules once in a while does not mean you abdicate your authority in the classroom—it just demonstrates that you are flexible.

JOURNALS

Keeping a journal can be applied to most subjects. I have found them useful as an avenue for children and teens to express themselves emotionally, as well as creatively. I have communicated with students who needed someone to be a receptive ear for their self-exploration, through prose and sometimes through poetry. In my sex education class, they were able to ask me things in the privacy of their journals that they felt embarrassed about asking in front of the whole class. I write a response to everyone. As one girl said, "I love my journal. It's like having a diary that talks."

But you must be very careful with these. Remember, you are not a trained counselor and should not be dispensing therapy but rather having conversations with your students. You must tell them that the journals are strictly confidential and will be shared with no one *unless* you feel they are in danger. By law, you must report a situation that endangers a minor. I had a girl living among nine crack addicts and had to have her removed from the home. I have become aware of potential suicides, as well as sexually abused youngsters. I reported these cases and felt comfort in knowing they were rescued.

Be careful what you say. I always respond to the journal with the understanding that a parent may read it the second the child leaves the house. I usually try to say what I suspect the parents want to say but have difficulty communicating. For example, one boy complained that his father is always screaming at him. From his description, the father sounded like a royal pain, but of course I couldn't say that. I acknowledged his feelings, and then offered the following suggestion: "It must feel terrible to feel you are being yelled at all the time. Perhaps you might try writing your dad a letter expressing how you feel. Sometimes parents don't realize their children are struggling. Good luck!"

KNOW WHEN YOU ARE OVERLY INVOLVED

Occasionally, a student will see you as a confidant, and it is up to you to learn how deeply to get involved and when to distance yourself.

I remember a dear student who would tell me her problems. I found myself spending too much time at home thinking about how I could help her. Some teachers live vicariously through their students, and they have to learn that when their favorite athlete doesn't get picked for the team, they shouldn't take it personally. The reality is that most students will distance themselves from you, but that rare student who needs to consume you has to be pushed back as gently as possible.

READ ALOUD TO YOUR STUDENTS

Anthony Alvarado, former New York City chancellor of schools, was our district superintendent. He was a brilliant educator who demonstrated a great lesson when he was an invited guest speaker at a monthly teacher conference. He came in to speak to us and instead took out a storybook and began to read to us. He read and read and, before long, we were all sitting there engrossed in the story. We adult educators did everything but suck our thumbs and twirl our hair. He asked us to read to our students as often as possible. He was not talking only about little children, but about teenagers as well. It is one of the most bonding techniques a teacher can share with her students.

GIANT CALENDAR

At one of my seminars, a teacher shared something with us that children enjoy very much. She had a giant yearly calendar in the back of the room on which she put everyone's birthday. She also included class trips, big test dates, special assemblies, and events, and she encouraged the children to circle dates they thought important enough to share with the class.

CELEBRATE BIRTHDAYS

Younger students love to have their birthdays acknowledged. Teens often pretend they don't care, but don't believe them for a minute. I suggest having a bulletin board with a list of everyone's birthdays so you can see at a glance whose birthday it is.

Don't forget to acknowledge those poor, deprived students whose birthdays fall on the holidays or during summer vacations. I'm still sore at my mother, who gave birth to me in July—depriving me of hearing my classmates sing "Happy Birthday" to me.

CATCH THE SPIRIT

I know you are tired at the end of the day, but it would be great if you could muster up a shot of adrenaline so you can show up at school rallies, plays, musical productions, dances, and so on. It makes your students feel they are very important to you. It shows the kids that you are part of the "family" and enjoy seeing them even when you don't have to. When you see them the next day, let them know you were impressed by their performances. I can guarantee huge beaming faces brimming with pride, as well as a sure way of building rapport. The best part is that you will probably have as much fun as your students. (If it's a dance, you might even be able to show them a step or two . . . but be prepared—they usually laugh at how teachers dance, so don't take it personally.)

At the risk of stating the obvious, let me caution you to be aware that if you attend an event where there is a chance of alcohol being snuck in, make sure you do not partake in the "fun." Teachers have lost their jobs because they were seen imbibing at a school football game.

"I Thought of You"

Occasionally, I would see something in a newspaper or magazine that I thought would be of interest to a particular student. I would clip it out and deliver it either before or after the class met. Once I bought a ceramic turtle at a yard sale (for a big 50 cents) for a boy in my class who was fixated on turtles. You would think I had bought him a new Mercedes by the grin on his face. He could not believe I had bought it especially for him for no reason. He told me he would save it for the rest of his life. It has probably turned up at his own yard sale, but it served a wonderful purpose at the time. It made someone feel important.

Another feel-good strategy is to mail that newspaper or magazine article to a student's home. What child doesn't love to see an envelope personally handwritten and addressed to him—rather than to mom or dad?

Morning Meetings

In the morning, let the children share anything they want to with the rest of the class. The children usually make some kind of an announcement. Someone might mention that her Uncle Mitch is coming from Oshkosh to visit or that his mother is having a baby. I have seen kids throw out a personal problem with which they needed help. They can relate a dream or merely a good laugh they had the night before. It is very bonding but usually works well with only a small group. It is up to you, the teacher, to make sure that everyone gets equal time. Beware: There is often that one student who wants to relate every detail of a 3-hour TV special.

CLASS SOLUTIONS

An extension of the morning meeting is what I call "the class solution." Very often if you are having a difficult time with your class, your class is having a difficult time with you and often the class is having a difficult time with each other. I have sometimes thrown in the towel and asked the class to join me in figuring out how to make the classroom feel safe for everyone. You would be surprised at the wisdom your students can bring to remedy the situation.

LOWDEN'S LIFE LESSONS
(OR, TEACHING WINNING WAYS)

(Of course you can substitute your name for mine in this strategy, but it may not be as alliterative. This is my quick course in "Nicen Up 101"—the course title is from my students.)

Sharing secrets that will make your students more agreeable to other teachers is something they might benefit from more than anything you teach from a textbook. Here are a few examples:

- I tell my kids never to admit that they didn't study when they get a 100 on a test. (Let the teacher think they studied their heads off.)
- I suggest that on the first day of classes they sit near the teacher and not run to a hidden corner because that makes a poor first impression.
- I stress that being "in a teacher's face" only makes the teacher hostile to them, and it is the teacher who has the power.
- I remind them that being nice—or using honey instead of vinegar—works! It is hard to dislike someone who is pleasant and cooperative, but it is really easy to dislike that disrespectful student who mouths off at you.
- I encourage them to do some damage control after they've been disrespectful to a teacher. They can approach the teacher, admit they "lost it," and ask if they can start all over with tomorrow being the first day.
- I teach them to use a lot of the communication strategies I describe in this book. Most of the strategies are appropriate for all ages.

Decorating Your Room . . . Again

I am sure the first day of school you have this lovely decorated room all ready to set the tone for your students. After a month or so, I have already suggested rotating seats (see page 15) because it changes the feel of the room. But something even more drastic is a pick-me-up that includes changing bulletin board colors and redecorating in general by putting different things on the boards. Don't we all look at our walls at home and want to paint them another color? Why not do a modified version of that with pretty construction paper? I am even going to go further and suggest bringing in fresh flowers occasionally. You can have a committee of "interior decorators" choose the redecorating. And please include boys as well as girls.

Assure Students You Will Tell Their Parents Something Wonderful

Many students go into cardiac arrest when parent-teacher conferences take place. Many of them know they are failing in school and dread the disapproval from their parents when they get home. It could be a terrifying moment, so to make everyone happy, I assure the students that I will find something wonderful to say about each and every one of them so that they don't get grounded for life. Every child has something special to be said about her—we just have to look a little further in some cases.

Thank Them for the Joy They Bring

You are going to have days that will make you thank your lucky star that you chose to be a teacher. You will be rewarded by seeing the light bulbs go on above their heads. Your students will tell you how they love you, and you will just have a great time. Why not share those good feelings with the very people who gave them to you by thanking them for the joy they brought you that day?

PART V

Building Confidence Through Earned Praise

When people feel good about themselves, they believe the sky's the limit. It is you and I who have to tap into those feelings of self-worth and facilitate growth. We have to help develop our students' belief in themselves before they can reach their full potential. Hopefully, some of these strategies will germinate the seeds of self-assurance.

CHAPTER SEVENTEEN

Self-Esteem Strategies

PRAISE, PRAISE, PRAISE—BUT DON'T OVERPRAISE

Remember, if you are too effusive, your compliments become meaningless. Sincere praise can only make a student feel good, but it is crucial that you praise for efforts and accomplishments rather than looks. (Unless, that is, your student is all decked out for a special occasion.)

When students work well with one another, express appreciation for their ability to cooperate. When a child hands in a drawing, focus on something special in it, such as use of color, composition, or imagination. When a student cracks a truly funny joke, laugh. That, too, is a form of praise.

Sometimes, a teacher might tell a student who wrote a nice poem, "Wow. You are the greatest poet!" But come on, little Rebecca is not Keats and she probably knows it, and so she may be uncomfortable with that compliment. However, telling her how beautiful her imagery is will likely be more meaningful and affirming.

Overpraising can have some real pitfalls. Giving too much praise and imposing expectations that are too high can be threatening to a student. The child who is told repeatedly, "You are always so good . . . I wish everyone was like you!" or "I know you will never disappoint me" can be overwhelmed and feel unfairly burdened. All children will at some time disappoint you; don't expect that even your star pupils will always be perfect.

ACKNOWLEDGE IMPROVEMENTS

One of the things we as educators must not forget is to acknowledge improvements—no matter how small. A little acknowledgment can go a long way toward raising self-esteem and getting the results you and your students desire. Notice how often we will call home to tell a parent that Harriet isn't doing her homework. But do we call home when Harriet starts to do her homework on a more regular basis? Usually not because homework being done on time should be expected.

But *soften up* and acknowledge that the improvement in her habits is not going unnoticed.

OVERGRADING

You have a wonderful student who shines, so you give her a grade of 100% or an A+ on her report card. But 100% means perfect, and so there is no room for improvement. The danger of giving students such a high grade is that the only way they can go on their next report card is down. I usually explain that to them, as well as to their parents. I know teachers who give 98s and 99s the first term, and it creates tremendous stress for the student to maintain that level. There is nothing wrong with a 95, and it does offer the opportunity for improvement.

CONFIDENCE GRADING

On the other side of the coin is the student who is barely passing, should fail, but yet tries so hard. I will often give the child a barely passing grade so as not to discourage him from keeping up a necessary level of determination and effort.

I do get disturbed when a teacher gives the same student a 90% because he tried hard. That is unfair. A 90 is well above average, and effort should not take precedence over quality. My 65 tells other teachers as well as my student that the work is marginal but passing. Anything else is really being dishonest to everyone and will only ensure the student gets a hard dose of reality down the road.

ENTHUSIASTIC CREDIT WHEN CREDIT IS DUE

In class, when someone contributes something truly wonderful, let him or her know.

I had a colleague, Yolanda, who, after I gave her a suggestion, would say, "Renee, that was a *fantastic* idea." I remember feeling a little surprised by her great effusion. And something else was going on. Her enthusiasm made me feel as though my ideas were second only to Einstein's. Her praise made me feel wonderful, so I started being more enthusiastic when my students came up with fine ideas of their own. Their glowing faces indicated that they were also believing in the value of their own ideas. Not a bad way to feel!

Remember that some students may be embarrassed, so tell them after class how impressed you were by them. Just be careful never to be patronizing or insincere. Here is a case where you must know your audience and be selective—and don't overpraise. The idea must really be exceptional.

PUT-UPS, NOT PUT-DOWNS

"If you have nothing nice to say, say nothing." This wisdom comes from my father (and probably yours, too).

Worthy compliments only make people feel good. Put-downs hurt even when the child says, "Words won't hurt me." You may be relieved when a student who is being picked on says, "I don't care." But don't believe the child for a second because words not only can hurt, they can leave scars.

RESPECT UNIQUENESS

This is a suggestion that I am sure some of you will disagree with. There is always a student who comes in with a pierced nose, wearing a strange get-up, and is just generally working hard at being different. If it is okay with his parents, and not against school rules, do not go on automatic and make negative comments. If it is a negative distraction, then you must do what you have to do to discourage it. Trust your gut reaction, and more often than not, when you get to know the "odd" student, he ends up being just a cool person who doesn't want to conform, but does want to be noticed.

LEADERS NEED TO FOLLOW

This is a problem that I have experienced but could never put my finger on why it bothered me until I heard a parent chastising a teacher because she was discouraging her child from "being a leader." Of course, we all want our students to have leadership qualities and good teachers nurture those qualities. However, sometimes there is a negative to this positive. When students work in groups, it is only natural for the leader to dictate what will and will not be done. It is often intimidating for the followers to disagree and that is where the stronger personalities have to learn how to be team players. It is up to us to see that all voices are heard and that the stronger personalities do not call all the shots and discourage others from offering their input.

DON'T RUSH TO CORRECT

Remember when you were a child and you stood up cheerfully to give your interpretation of an answer you just knew the teacher wanted? And then the teacher said, "Wrong. Sit down. Who can give me the right answer?" Can you remember how your face stung with embarrassment?

What *I* say is, "That's not quite what I had in mind, but that's an interesting way to look at it" or "That was a good guess." Simply dismissing an incorrect answer can intimidate the child and discourage him or her from volunteering an answer in the future for fear of being humiliated.

CALL HOME FOR THE "AVERAGE" STUDENT

There are students who always do average work. They are neither Madam Curies nor Charles Mansons. They are just average students who come to school and do their work.

Notice how those who do well earn praise and high grades and acknowledgment, and those who misbehave earn a telephone call to their parents. Well, every once in a while, I call the home of a student who puts in great effort. I will tell the parent how I enjoy his child and what a pleasure it is to have her in my class. The parent usually asks, "Okay, what's wrong?" After I assure him that that was my only motive, I usually have a beaming parent and the next day a beaming student. Everyone profits from this—and it takes only a couple of minutes of my time.

"I KNEW YOU COULD DO IT" (AND MORE)

"I knew you could do it" is a wonderful thing to hear, but sometimes it's not enough. Not too long ago, I was asked to debate an issue before a large professional group. I used to get terribly nervous debating before a large audience. I finally decided I had to overcome this fear. I accepted an engagement and prepared (and worried) for a month. The big night came and it went great. When I came home and told my family all went well, they said, "We knew you could do it." What I really wanted to ask was, "Why did you think I could do it?" But that would be fishing for compliments, and modesty prevents that.

So when my students accomplish something they believed they couldn't do, I tell them why I knew they could. For instance, I had one girl who feared speaking aloud in front of the class, and I told her that I knew she could do it because she has so much to say and such a warm way of speaking.

A LITTLE WHITE LIE

I don't want you to read this book and walk away saying I told you to lie. However, a fib is different from a lie. Okay, maybe it isn't, but sometimes we have to cross our fingers behind our backs to save a child from pain or embarrassment.

For instance, I once told a boy that I thought his haircut was nice when in fact it looked as if the barber had had one drink too many. If you are so honest that an untruth cannot escape your lips, try to give a noncommittal response like, "It sure is unique."

When I ask my husband if he thinks I am prettier than Angelina Jolie, he says, "Renee, there's no contest!" or "What a silly question!" I take that as I want.

"You're a Late Bloomer"

This may or may not be a fib, but it can raise the self-confidence of students.

I loathe tracking and ache for the students who are assigned to the "slow" track. It has to be humiliating to them. So I will tell my students that having read their records, I believe them to be under-achievers. I explain that somewhere along the way, they just weren't ready and in most cases that is the truth. I have had students believe they were capable of much more and—lo and behold!—they allow themselves to learn so much more. I have seen scores skyrocket, and, more important, I have heard them tell others that they are late bloomers and are more capable than others believe them to be.

Tracking

One of my principals used to give us lectures on why it was so important to raise the self-esteem of our students. At the same time, she had the school divided into "smart" classes and "not smart" classes. I don't care what euphemism one uses. By assigning the number 1 to the top class and 10 to the bottom class, you are defining these students to themselves and to others. So I have to use the afore-said "Late Bloomers" strategy for these bottom groups.

The argument for tracking is, "All the students know who the smart kids are anyway." That is fine. No one complains about being too smart. That's why I have no objection to honors classes. But it is the middle and bottom classes that do not need to be publicly defined. Using a room number serves the same purpose. It defines a group without defining its abilities. Instead of 4–10, it would be 4–301.

One year a new teacher suggested we put students in Grades 7–9 in the same English class with all reading levels represented. I didn't think it would work but *Darn!* these new teachers are smart, so I went along with her plan. We were lucky enough that year to be involved in an experimental program and had about 18 students per class. As a result, we were able to grade each student according to his or her own abilities.

What we saw, amazingly, was that a student who had a low read-ing score might be very verbal and contribute as much to a discus-sion as a high scorer. The kids all helped one another and it was awesome. Most of you aren't lucky enough to have such small groups, but if you are, go ahead and try something like this. Our luck lasted only a year. The funding dried up and we were back to 30 per class, and a class such as the one I just described cannot work with such a huge academic and chronological gap.

SOME OF US CAN'T SPELL

Here I am, about to encourage you to have separate spelling groups. Remember, I'm the same person who loathes tracking, and you ask if I am really telling you to have two different groups? Yup. Some folks are simply terrible spellers, even though they excel in advanced calculus (and then there are people like me: I can spell, but need all my fingers to add up numbers!). I stress to my students that spelling is not directly related to intelligence—that some of us are better spellers than others. I point out that Einstein was an allegedly horrendous speller, and he didn't do too badly! I then give my students the opportunity to choose a spelling group that they feel would be appropriate for their ability. I will ask, "Who is a so-so speller?" There is always a brave soul who will raise his hand, and then the rest follow suit. They know their spelling words will be a little easier, or that perhaps they will get fewer words to memorize. By openly discussing poor spelling skills, I destigmatize it, and those with trouble can focus in a more relaxed manner.

WONDERFUL COMMENTS ON PAPER

Every student's heart skips a beat as the papers on which they worked so laboriously are being returned. What is the first thing they see from 20 yards away? *Red ink!* We all associate that color with criticism. But there is nothing that says criticism has to be all negative and that we cannot find something kind to say. Even when a paper has more red ink on it than black, you can tell a student that there are some really good ideas here or how much you are looking forward to the revision. Putting a happy face on the top of the paper is fine, but please scrap the frowning faces, unless that's what you want to see on your students' faces. You also might try using purple or green ink once in a while.

POST EACH STUDENT'S WORK

Many teachers believe that the "best" papers should be exhibited on the bulletin boards. But there are always those children who don't get 100%, or have terrible handwriting, or just produce average work. Those students never see their work up on the board, even though they have tried as hard as they could and worked to their full potential. I feel we should acknowledge all of our students, not only the ones who score high on tests.

One day I casually mentioned that I needed papers to put up on the bulletin board, and if they just dropped them on my desk, I would hang them up. I just knew it would be those same perfect papers . . . but was I wrong. It surprised me that the students who often did not do well dropped their papers for me to exhibit. It made it clear that everyone needs to be acknowledged and showed how much they wanted their "names in lights." I have seen students take extra pains to write as neatly as possible so their work will look good.

Often teachers will hang up papers riddled with errors. I still display these papers, but the bulletin board is labeled "Work in Progress." I want the student to recognize that his or her work is not finished merely because it is being displayed. It is also important because parents or administrators seeing papers needing work might think that they were acceptable.

"I GOT A 97%! WHAT DID YOU GET?"

Have you noticed that it is only the students who get very high grades who yell across the room to another, "Hey Cindy, what did you get on the test?" Very seldom does a student with a failing paper do that.

I tell my students that they can tell their own grade, but they are not to ask about a classmate's grade in front of others. I assure them that if their friend has a good grade, we will all know, and if not, silence will be enough. This is why I try to minimize competition for grades. (See also The Sanctuary on page 52.)

PART VI

Safety

We are living in a time when school children are exhibiting violence that was unheard of years ago and parents are suing schools and teachers in record numbers. I wish this were not happening, but it is. You need to know how to protect your students, yourself, and your school. The following tips will make you a little wiser in the art of self-protection, and the long-term effect will be a safeguard for the students you care so much about.

CHAPTER EIGHTEEN

Personal, Physical, and Professional Safety

TO TOUCH OR NOT TO TOUCH

I have to be really careful about what I write here because of how sensitive this issue has become. Sometimes I hear comments such as, "A kindergarten teacher can't even wipe a child's runny nose because she will be sued." I hardly believe that, and I think anyone who is in the classroom knows her safety boundaries early on.

I am more concerned with older students who are going through puberty and are uncomfortable with their sexuality. Teachers are in a power position and may feel completely comfortable touching students, but in more cases than not, the student will feel uncomfortable being touched.

We had a teacher who used to ask the fifth-grade girls for a hug. He was a very nice teacher, but I had to tell him that his behavior was inappropriate. He was outraged at me and accused me of being out of line, but those girls who had complained to me thanked me for my action. (See Confronting Other Teachers on page 153).

FACE THE DOOR

When you are trying to find the ideal furniture arrangement, be careful where you place your desk. I had mine with my back to the door, and our security guard suggested that this was not a good idea. You are the adult in the room and are responsible for your students' safety. You need to see who comes in and goes out of your room at all times, and having your back to the door makes that impossible. Be extra careful to face the door while you are alone in your classroom grading papers.

NEVER RELEASE A STUDENT TO A STRANGER

Today so many children are from divorced homes. Many custody provisions involve extended family members as well as immediate family and it can get confusing. You must make sure that everyone who is authorized to pick up a child has written consent from the custodial parent. There should be a custody order on file to protect you. Never release a child to someone you do not know unless it has been clearly stated that it is alright to do so. I suggest you know all this information from day one.

NEVER THROW A STUDENT OUT OF YOUR ROOM

If it hasn't happened yet, it will . . . you have a student who is driving you to the brink of homicide and driving everyone else crazy. The only way to alleviate the problem is to go on automatic and kick him out of the room. Sounds great, but you cannot do that because he may end up where he doesn't belong. This could spell deep trouble for you. You must have a specific destination and have someone escort him there. You can ask a colleague, or if there is no one near you, you can either send a trusted student with a pass to escort the disrupter to the office or you can get the dean or call out the militia.

DON'T BREAK UP FIGHTS

This is something I learned the hard way. I taught in a very tough school where fighting with fists was the preferred way to settle disputes. I broke up many fights, and then one year, two boys were about to kill each other and I got in the middle and suddenly there

I was, seeing stars! The good news is that I broke up the fight, and even better, those two combatants felt so guilty they practically waited on me hand and foot for months.

When there is a fight, your first response is to get help. You are not a trained referee, and the end result is you can get seriously hurt. You should send another student to the office immediately and use your cell phone to call the office. Some of you might be lucky enough to have a school with a phone in the room, so use it and don't risk injury.

SCREEN THE VIDEOS

I once rewarded my class with a fun movie (before ratings) that I was told was appropriate for middle schoolers. I trusted the judgment of a colleague and showed it to my class. When it opened with scantily clad college students running around, I knew I was in trouble! I feared what the kids were going to tell their parents, but fortunately, the movie stayed just barely within the bounds of decency. Always preview a movie you are going to show to a class and check with your school to make sure it is on the "approved list" if your school has one. Fortunately movies have ratings now, but still do not take a chance showing something a parent or student might find objectionable.

YOUR SCHOOL'S EMERGENCY PLAN

In the beginning of the year, you will get a detailed plan for emergencies. When the bells ring for an emergency drill, it is very scary to many children. (I have been known to get a bit nervous myself.) One doesn't always know for sure whether it is just a drill or a real crisis. To prevent any accidents or confusion, be sure you have the route to safety memorized. It is a good idea for you to try the route before there is a drill to be sure you can confidently (and most of all calmly) get the kids safely outside.

Another thing is be sure to post the plan showing the exits specified for your room. Someone new may be using your room and will not know where to go.

THE CAFETERIA

One of my readers reminded me that the cafeteria is a place where there are many possibilities for health hazards, as well as poor manners. I am sure we have all had the experience of being on cafeteria patrol. If not, consider yourself lucky. The cafeteria is often noisy, messy, and okay I will say it . . . smelly.

Children often drop garbage. We want to avoid a major confrontation in an often volatile environment; so when you catch a kid slipping her empty milk container under the table try a one-on-one (see One-on-One on page 95). You ask the student if you may speak with her privately and then ask her, politely, to pick up the container she dropped. Make sure you thank her after she picks it up. It might be a good idea to talk to your class about cafeteria etiquette. Kids hate the idea of picking up "trash" for others, so it is up to us to raise their consciousness about what makes a pleasant room for "dining." You can also personalize it and explain that the custodian gets upset when there is a mess left by them for him to clean up. If your custodian is willing, it would be great if he spoke to your class.

KEEP THE DOOR OPEN

When you find yourself alone in the classroom with a student (of either gender), be sure to leave the door ajar. This really saddens me, but it is a reality that has to be addressed in these times. There have been cases when students have falsely accused teachers of misconduct and there are cases in which there was, in fact, misconduct. Since it will always be "your word against hers or his," protect yourself by not being alone in a room with the door closed. If a student wants to speak with you, it is a good idea to step outside in the hall so there will be no misinterpretation of intention. People like to gossip and you do not want to find yourself the source of it.

NEVER LEAVE CLASSES UNATTENDED

You have to go to the bathroom for a minute, you just want to run something off on the copy machine, or you just want to make a quick phone call. You have the kids working quietly and you know you can trust them . . . WRONG!! You are responsible for your class and leaving them alone, even for a minute, can be catastrophic. A colleague of mine once ran to the office for just a few minutes and when she got back a student was having a life-threatening asthma attack. Your best students can act totally different when there is a live audience of 25 to show off for and no teacher to stop them. Never take the chance because you can be inviting a lawsuit as well as endangering the children in your charge.

Find out from your principal what the protocol is for leaving your room. In some states an adult can watch your class for you, while in other states, only a licensed teacher can be in charge. It is also inadvisable, not to mention unfair, to ask a colleague who has her own class to keep an eye on your room.

You Are Neither a Pharmacist nor a Doctor

I always carried aspirin in my purse, and when I was a new teacher, one of my students complained of a headache. Not realizing that I was never to dispense medication, I gave her a couple of aspirins. She had a reaction (nothing serious, just an upset stomach) and started crying that the pills made her sick and she wanted to go home. Luckily the parent was not bothered, but if the parent had wanted to, she could have made a big deal out of it. Even worse, the student could have had a more adverse reaction and there could have been serious side effects. Send a sick student to the nurse or call home to ask the parent to take your student home. Just a reminder, you should be aware of students who need medication and if you can, you should remind them to take it. Remember everything regarding medication should be in writing and signed by the parents. All schools have their own policy and you should be sure that you know it.

Another thing to steer clear of is dispensing medical advice. Some of us believe certain herbs and vitamins are beneficial, others think no one should eat red meat, and others think heat is good on a bruise while others think ice is. All of these are your "unexpert" opinions and should not be shared with your students.

Do Not Drive Your Students in Your Car

You see that dear student glumly standing by the front door. He missed the bus and looks totally lost. Being the good person you are, you put him in your car and drive him home. Great scenario . . . but it could have a bad ending. I suggest unless you have a written permission slip to have a student in your car, do not take the chance. You could get into an accident and your student could get injured. You can miss a parent who comes to claim your student and then is sure you kidnapped her. Your passenger can get very ill and you may not know what to do. You can even have a malicious child who can accuse you of doing all kinds of terrible things. So think twice before putting yourself in this situation. Again, I stress that lawsuits are too commonplace and even good intentions could bring one against you and your school.

REPORT EVERY ACCIDENT

Little Barry trips and holds his arm and whines a little. Two seconds later, he gets up and starts running around again. Common sense tells us he is probably fine, but let me warn you, we have to discard common sense and go for the long shot. Barry may seem absolutely fine and then by the time he gets home, his arm (that looked fine to you) may be twice the size and fractured. Don't take the chance of assuming it is nothing. I have seen minor scrapes become infected and minor bumps on the head prove to be mild concussions. Document the accident and be sure the student has an active part in reporting it. It is important that you make the student aware that running around can cause these consequences. I will repeat what I said earlier in the book—DOCUMENT! DOCUMENT! DOCUMENT!

TRUST YOUR GUT FEELINGS AND FOLLOW INSTINCTS

Too often we do not follow our gut feelings, but instead, allow logic and reasoning to win out. I have had times when I felt uncomfortable about a student. Often I would read a journal and my instincts told me the student was in some danger, even though the student didn't say so. More often than not, my gut feeling was right. Occasionally I was too late to ameliorate a dangerous or unhealthy situation. But remember also, if they are not going to talk to you, there is only so much you can do. I also suggest you share your concerns with the guidance counselor so at least you did your duty by reporting it. Better safe than sorry.

Go Home Already!

Many of us are delighted to have peace and quiet at the end of the day and a little time to catch up with all the tasks we have to do for the next day. (Of course, nonteachers think we work only half a day, but never mind, I will address that later.) Again, I have to be realistic and address the problem of security that plagues our schools. I have known teachers who have had their purses stolen by intruders. It isn't a good idea to be alone in an empty school where you can be a sitting target for someone who is up to no good. In my school, the custodians politely kicked us out of the building after 5 o'clock. They did not want to have to worry about us. At times if we needed to work late, we would pair up so we would never be alone in the room. You can rotate rooms or work where it is convenient for both of you, but do not stay too late after school.

PART VII

Using Your Support System

T eaching is an "interdependent" profession. Without the help of parents, fellow teachers, administrators, and support staff, your job would be overwhelmingly complex. You need to develop strong relationships with these people to make a school work. Our profession, though very rewarding, can also be difficult and frustrating. What is important is teamwork, and for your team to be successful, you must be a team player. Remember: Although there may be disagreements, you are all on the same side with the same goals. You all want your students to succeed.

CHAPTER NINETEEN

Working With Parents

MEET PARENTS RIGHT AWAY

Parents are a wonderful asset and certainly should be utilized. Very often parents never even meet the teacher until Open School Day or after being summoned. I think it is very important for you to put faces to the parents of your students. They also get to meet you and see how terrific you are. As a parent, I always wanted to meet my daughter's teachers, but I rarely did because of my busy schedule. One year, her teacher invited all the parents to come to school one evening. She told us her objectives, gave us a short demonstration lesson, and asked us if there was anything she should know about our child. Because she scheduled a specific day and time, we were all there. It is like your friend who says, "Drop over any time." You rarely do, unless she sets a specific time. So you might try that with your students' parents.

SEND HOME AN INTRODUCTION

Many parents cannot spare the time to come to school except when required, so a nice touch is to send home a letter of introduction. Tell them about yourself and what you hope to accomplish this year with their child. Encourage them to not hesitate to call you at school if they have any concerns. Here I would suggest you give them the school number rather than your home number because some parents call for every little thing. You might close your letter by asking if they have any insights into their child that would make his or her educational experience more productive. Now, what parent wouldn't enjoy getting a letter like that? And starting off on such a good foot surely can't hurt.

ACCOMMODATE PARENTS

Many students have parents who work outside of the home or have schedules that make it difficult, if not impossible, to speak with you during the school day. Meeting with teachers is often frustrating for them. We all know that speaking in person has much more impact than a phone call or note home. It is not required that you come in early to speak to an anxious parent, nor is it required that you stay after school for the same purpose, but if you can, try to accommodate them. Sometimes just meeting them gives you insights into your student and lets the parent know how seriously you take their child's education.

INFORM PARENTS EARLY ON

When writing this book, I addressed many parent groups and asked for input into what they want from a teacher. Something that was repeated over and over was their desire to be informed early on if their children aren't doing well. Many parents are shocked when they find out their child isn't doing her class work. Parents often criticize teachers unfairly and we often blame them for not doing their share, but the reality is we have to work together. Parents should be encouraged to check their child's homework each night to make sure it is being done; but that being said, we have to make doubly sure that they know when there are problems. A quick note or phone call to alert them of potential problems serves the child, the parent, and, of course, you. Don't wait for the mandated notices you have to send. When the report card comes with less than desirable grades, the shock will have been averted by that informative phone call.

Another thing to keep in mind is that many parents told me that they appreciate knowing in advance of any big projects their children have.

Tear on the Dotted Line

When we send something home that we want parents to read, one idea is to put a tear strip at the end of the note. Have the parent sign and return it with the student. Then the tear strip can be used as a raffle ticket. This will motivate children to bring home newsletters or important notices because of the reward it offers . . . and we all know rewards are the best motivator.

Parents and the Internet

We are a cyberspace society. The Internet can be a great way to communicate with your students, and it is also a wonderful way to communicate with parents. On the first day, have your students and parents fill out a questionnaire and in it request the parents' e-mail addresses and ask them if they want to be kept abreast of exams, due dates for assignments, class trips, and any other information you might think would be of use to them. If you are very ambitious you might put out a newsletter for the parents and/or students once a week or once a month, depending on how overloaded you are with work. E-mail is a nice way for you to communicate with the parents and it is usually a lot quicker than a telephone call or a conference. (And it also thwarts the phone tag game.) School systems have that technology in place . . . make sure to update regularly! Parents use this technology as a lifeline to keep track of what their kids are doing in school (or *not* doing as the case may be). If you do not update these sites regularly, principals often have to hear calls from frustrated parents who will call out teachers by name who don't "participate."

I also must stress here that sometimes a face to face is needed. Typed words often lose their impact and sometimes they even lose their meaning through misinterpreted nuances.

Getting Parents Involved

Every school has active parents whom everyone else counts on to do all the work. However, it is important to encourage all parents to be involved in their child's schooling. Some parents are actually intimidated by that expectation and back away. Calling parents once in a while can make them feel comfortable with you. You might ask if they would join the class on a trip, or share some time helping with reading groups, or perhaps talk to the class about the work they do. However, before you invite one to lecture, ask your student how he or she feels about it. Some kids are embarrassed by their parent's presence, whereas others are thrilled. When the parents do help, a short thank-you note is always appropriate and thoughtful.

SPECIAL RELATIVE DAY

A nice idea is to invite other family members, as well as parents, to visit your student in class. Grandparents are as much fun to watch as your students. They are easy to spot because they don't take their eyes off their grandchild nor the smile off their faces. A special uncle, who does funny things with his ears, is always fun for his niece to show off. You can call it "Bring Your Relative to School Day" and make lots of people happy.

CALL *BOTH* PARENTS

How many times do teachers say, "Okay, that's it! I am going to call your *mother*!" I always believed that parenting involved two parents. Yes, sometimes there is only one parent, but often there are two. As a mother, I feel it is an unfair burden if a teacher assumes I am the only parent responsible for our child. I don't want my child, or anyone else's, to get the impression that the responsibility all falls on Mother.

We should tell our students we are going to call home, or call a parent. Always "calling the mother" is unfair to mothers and implies fathers don't share the joint responsibility. Worse yet, it causes our students to internalize erroneous gender roles.

It is a good idea for you to find out with whom your student lives. It could be a grandparent, foster parent, or even an institution.

STUDENTS AT PARENT CONFERENCES?

Whether students should be present at parent conferences is a debatable question to which I can answer both yes and no and be correct.

This is really a judgment call. Many teachers demand that their students come with their parents, while others forbid it. I do neither. I tell my students that my practice is to speak to their parents alone, but they may feel free to join in after our conversation. I tell them that in advance so they do not think I am saying horrible things about them. In fact, when they join us I will say something glowing so they all leave on an "up."

The reason I want to confer with parents in private is because sometimes the *parents* may not be able to talk openly in front of the child. Parents may be contemplating a divorce, there may be a death in the family, or they may feel out of control regarding their child—any number of things that could make the child's presence inhibiting. When they're all talked out, ask the parents if you may discuss what they have shared with you with their child now, or perhaps at a later date.

I had a student, Penny, who was nearly perfect, and I didn't think I had to talk to the mother privately, but because I had told the class I do that with everyone, I had to. Well, in that conference I learned that Penny was anorexic. Penny wanted it to remain a secret, but her mother thought it was too important not to share with me. And the mother admitted that she would not have told me this in her daughter's presence.

As I said, many teachers feel it is necessary for the child to be sitting there so everything will be out in the open but will it really be?

TEACHER AS MIDDLEMAN

Parent conferences can be traumatic for our students. They are sure you are going to tell their parents that they are axe murderers in the making, and that goes for honor students as well as those who are struggling. For some reason our students see private conferences with parents as a conspiracy against them. However, something else has to be understood. The conference doesn't have to be only what you want to talk to the parents about, nor what the parent wants to talk to you about. This is an opportunity for you to ask your students if there is anything they want you to relate to their parents before the day of the conference. Often kids can't tell their parents certain things for fear they will upset them. I had a student whose parents never would help with her homework and she wanted them to know how badly she needed their help. Having that information enabled me to bring the topic up surreptitiously. I told them that it was very important that all parents help with homework and I really stressed the importance. They never knew the concern was their daughter's and the bottom line was they showed a great interest in her work after that.

PARENT-TEACHER CONFERENCE MANAGEMENT

A joyful sight to a teacher is a classroom filled with parents on Parent Conference Night. Since they may have to wait a long time for you, you might have their child's work available for them to look at, as well as a sign-in sheet so you can see who was there. You should have the syllabus, grading formula, and the class rules for the parents to look at while they are waiting for you. A good idea is to leave out paper or index cards and ask them to write any questions they will want addressed. When the time comes to meet with you, they have questions at hand and it will speed up the process a bit. I wish I had a tip for how to make parents aware that there are others waiting to talk to you. I never could master the art of telling a parent . . . "ENOUGH!!"

ASSURING PARENTS

Parents love their kids. They may not always like their behavior and may even say terrible things about them, but don't you dare think of agreeing with them! Often parents, like their children, need to know you are on their side.

I have had terribly hostile parents come up to me and I would react in kind. Nothing was accomplished because we were both defending ourselves. Once you let them know you are not attacking their parenting skills, one layer of the armor goes down. I had a mother come to me with a real attitude. Just as we were about to square off, I put my hand on hers, and said, "Ms. Johnson, we both care about Jack. I know you teach him right from wrong, and please know he is very special to me, too." Suddenly, it was as if I were talking to a new parent. I found out many painful things I needed to know about Jack that explained his erratic behavior. She shared information she never would have, had she perceived me as an adversary.

Another strategy is to say things to the student in front of the parent such as the following:

"You probably think your parents and I think we know it all and are always telling you what to do."

"Do you know how hard it is to be a parent?"

"Do you know that your parents go to bed at night and worry about you?"

Parents love it (and you), and some children do gain insight.

THE DEFENSIVE PARENT

Do any of you remember when you were a child and the teacher made a phone call home and you knew you were in trouble? Well, bad news: Now you are the teacher and you may still get in trouble for a phone call home. You may call enabling parents who will immediately put you on the defensive and not believe a word you say. You may hear something like, "Little Helen said you are picking on her for nothing and so is every other teacher, and I want to know what you are going to do about it." I always expected, naively, that a parent would support me when I had difficulty with a child. However, when I became a parent, I too knew I had given birth to the perfect angel. If there was a complaint about her from a teacher, my gut reaction was a desire to inflict physical harm on him for practicing blasphemy. Fortunately, I learned to listen to and support the teacher and work toward solutions that would better the situation.

Please be prepared for the parents who enable their children by always defending them, right or wrong. The reality is that most parents are wonderfully cooperative and helpful, but I want you to be prepared for the occasional difficult one.

PARENTS AND HOMEWORK

Very often, well-meaning parents do their child's homework. They seem to have a hard time drawing the line between helping and doing. If you notice the caliber of a student's work seems to be above her ability, you might speak to the parent. I encourage parents not to do work *for* their child but, rather, *with* their child. It is important for a parent to check homework, help the child prepare for exams, and help explain something the child doesn't understand. But doing the homework for one's child, when she doesn't understand it, is a disservice to that child.

I might also mention here again that your assignments make a statement about you. They tell whether you are smart, boring, creative, unrealistic, or lazy.

CHILDREN AS DREAM FULFILLERS

As parents, we all have dreams for our children. Often they are the dreams we couldn't fulfill for ourselves, or they are dreams that we truly believe will make our child happy. Sometimes, we teachers have to rescue our students from their own parents' expectations. All children have limitations, and too often a parent refuses to see them and pushes a child too far. I have seen students suffering from depression because they feel they are disappointing their parents. No child should be made to feel that way, and you have to make that perfectly clear to a parent who you feel is creating this problem. I suggest you have the guidance counselor handle it.

Stuyvesant High School in New York City is one of the most prestigious high schools in the country. Needless to say, there is fierce competition among applicants to the school. It specializes in math and science, and, too often, I see students who have average aptitudes in these subjects cram, take expensive courses, and stress out because their parents will be upset if they don't get in. I have also had other students who are very bright but hated math and science, yet chose to go to that school because it fulfilled their parents' dreams rather than their own.

PARENTS *KNOWING* MORE THAN YOU

Parents who have finished high school might think that their experiences make them experts in the field of teaching. They will tell you what you are doing wrong and sometimes even forget to praise you when you are doing something right.

Don't get defensive, unless of course they become utterly offensive, in which case it might be a good idea to have a discussion in the presence of your principal. Just smile and thank them for their advice. Ever notice that when Johnny can't read, it's because of the terrible teacher; but when he is a scholar, it's because he inherited his parents' great genes?

THE BLAME GAME

When researching ideas for this book, I would be remiss if I didn't share my epiphany with you after talking to hundreds of teachers. We all know only too well how parents blame us for all the ills of the world. We obviously cannot teach their children the way they think we should, we get too much vacation . . . you name it, we take the rap. That is indeed a problem, but I notice that teachers sometimes do the same thing. How often do we blame parents for rude children? How often do we accuse the parents of not caring, or being too busy working? (See Don't Stereotype below.) That is just as unfair. If we have not met the parents we should not blame the actions of their children on them. I have taught thousands of students and I have yet to meet parents who didn't believe they were doing the best job they could. I have seen kids act out and be disrespectful and yet when the parent comes in bewildered, I understand why. That very student is respectful to his parent and hardly the same child I know. That is not to say that many students are indeed as rude in front of their parents as they are in class. Often parents will shirk it off with, "Oh, he is just acting like a kid," or worse, tell you they just don't know what to do and admit they are out of control. Then we know there is a real problem and the school counselor should be advised.

Sometimes peer pressure brings out the worst in kids, and we should stop blaming the parents without being sure they are at fault. Hey, we can always blame the administration or the union!

DON'T STEREOTYPE

Often, without meaning to, we stereotype families and make assumptions we shouldn't. We use labels such as "single parent," "low income," "working mothers," or "latchkey kids," and we conclude that these parents will be hard to reach and will not be involved. These parents care about their children as much as you or I. Unfortunately, because of their situations, they are often not able to be as involved as they would like to be, and so we have to make every effort to engage them and not draw a negative conclusion about them. Something else you might consider: Some of these parents have so much confidence in the teacher that they think their input isn't valued, when in fact it should be encouraged!

BEWARE OF THE ANSWERING MACHINE

Believe it or not, I actually began teaching before the advent of the answering machine. (And I am still alive.) When we need to call home, we now hear singing messages, humorous messages, and unending messages before we can leave our own message for what we hope will be a parent. It is tempting fate to leave a message in which you tell parents that their child is in deep trouble. Would you blame your student for "accidentally" pushing the erase button?

I suggest you leave a message merely stating that you would like to speak to a parent. Use as upbeat a voice as you can muster. Then say that you will assume they did not get the message if they do not call back and that you will try again later. After all, how many accidents can a student have before someone gets suspicious?

*67

You are home and you want to call a parent because you tried all day in school and the parent wasn't available to take your call. You have learned from experience that if you leave messages, they magically disappear, or for some reason the answering machine was broken when you called. I have two explanations. Your student got home and deleted the message knowing she was in trouble, or the parent said he did not get it because he just didn't want to deal with a complaining teacher.

I suggest calling home in the evening, but I know you don't want your phone number showing up on caller ID, so I suggest using the teacher saving *67. This prevents the family from getting your phone number, as it will be blocked. Of course every time this book is updated there is another electronic improvement and one such improvement is that blocked calls aren't received, but it is worth a try.

CHAPTER TWENTY

Working With the School Support Team

PARTNER WITH THE COUNSELORS

Please be understanding when one of your students is called out of class by her counselor or school psychologist. Remember that if a child is troubled, chances are she won't be able to concentrate on your lesson. More often than not, a counselor tries to pick a time to talk with kids when it is least disruptive; however, if you feel a counselor is using your class time too often, plan a time to speak to her privately and air your concern. One thing we lose sight of is that the counselor is there to help these students. Our concern has to be for the whole child, and that includes her mental health as well as her academic growth.

COVER YOUR BACK . . . WHEN TO CONSULT YOUR SCHOOL COUNSELOR OR PSYCHOLOGIST

It's always important to document your actions in order to protect yourself professionally and to remember that you are not a trained mental health specialist. Along the same line, it is imperative to report any concerns you may have about a child immediately to his counselor. It is better for everyone to err on the side of being neurotic versus hoping everything is okay when it really isn't. By letting the counselor know of a concern, you are protecting the child and allowing the counselor to do her job. It is you who sees your students every day, whereas a counselor sees them only occasionally. You are on the front line—pull in your backup! Your input and concern are appreciated!

CONFLICT RESOLUTION

Conflict resolution and peer mediation are two programs being implemented in schools all over the country in which teachers, students, and parents go through a training program for several days. The result is that students are empowered to help other students settle disputes. A teacher is present, but two trained student mediators work with two (or more) disputants to prevent disagreements from escalating. They use many of the strategies mentioned here, using rules agreed upon before the mediation session. If your school does not have such a program, I suggest you encourage them to implement one.

COOPERATIVE TEACHER INPUT

Several of my colleagues and I used to arrive at school an hour early to share concerns and strategies regarding our students. It is helpful when a teacher informs you that a student has some personal problems or can share some information about his interaction with classmates. It's always helpful to know where your students need enrichment. However, you must remember not to share specific information that would be violating a confidence. An example would be the girl in my class who was upset because she was pregnant and didn't want anyone to know. I felt it inappropriate to share that information. However, I told my colleagues that she had some pressing personal problems.

BUDDY TEACHER

Sometimes every trick we have tried doesn't work, and we feel ourselves about to go on "automatic" and fear we will say and do things we will regret—like murder! A good idea is to prearrange with another teacher to be a "buddy." This teacher will take a student out of your room for you, or you can merely tell your student to go to your colleague's room. You might find a student particularly resistant, in which case you'd give him a choice. "Either you go to Mr. Tenney's room or you go to the dean or principal!" They usually opt for choice number one and they are surprisingly well behaved there. Don't take it personally. It is not unlike the young child who will eat liver at a friend's house but will fast indefinitely at yours.

OTHER TEACHERS' SUCCESSES

Sometimes we have students who just don't listen, and if they do listen, they aren't necessarily hearing what we are saying. Sometimes we have entire classes where everything you do seems to fall flat. We all know that happens and too often we keep it our own little dark secret because we don't want to admit that the teacher across the hall who has some of your students is winning them over. Sometimes we have to swallow our pride and admit defeat. Remember, we can't win 'em all and what works for you might not work for someone else and vice versa. It is the vice versa I am going to talk about now.

When you see a teacher having great success with a class or having a difficult student practically eating out of her hand, ask her what it is that she is doing right. If you are confident you might ask her what you might be doing wrong. Sometimes something so simple might make the difference in a class. I did that and the teacher told me that my problem kid becomes wonderful when you talk to him one on one. I did that, and things changed for the better. Had I not gotten that tip, I would be still looking for a solution.

CONFRONTING OTHER TEACHERS

This one is a toughie! Students will often confide in me about difficulties they are having with another teacher. Usually I will try to mediate the situation and arm my student with strategies, many of which I've presented already. It is important for your students to know that sometimes life is not fair, and that extends into the classroom. Be very careful not to speak badly about another teacher because that is highly unprofessional. I have heard students gripe about certain teachers, and I know their gripes are legitimate. I explain that in the real world we are always going to have to deal with difficult people, and school is an early training ground. Our students cannot just explode if they don't like it when one teacher takes off three points for a missed homework although another teacher doesn't.

As an advocate for students, we are remiss if we do not defend the child who is legitimately being unfairly treated after trying all reasonable actions. You must then intercede and try to mediate the situation with your colleague. If you cannot do that, and I know it is difficult, speak to an administrator. You may not win a popularity contest with that teacher, but you will have done what we are all paid to do and that is to be an advocate for students.

NO GOSSIPING ABOUT YOUR STUDENTS

This sounds so obvious, but it is so difficult to carry out. Teachers head into the teachers' lounge and within five minutes, we are talking about our students. It is very difficult not to express our anger, our disappointment, our frustration, our wrath, our animosity, and whatever other negative feelings we might have at that moment. Be careful not to pass along a negative story about a specific child unless you do it in a positive way that may result in solutions to the problem. Sometimes people hear you talking about a child and the story somehow ends up in the ears of the parents, who then (rightfully so) get upset that their child was the topic of gossip. In a previous tip (see Ignore Reputation on page 87), I told you to form your own opinion of a student. Hearing teachers badmouth kids does prejudice your expectations. If there is anything confidential, take it out of the lounge and into a private space. Even when talking with a counselor, it is best to go into his office and shut the door before discussing the problem.

TEACHER COMPETITION

In all professions, there is competition among coworkers, and teaching is no exception. You need to know your audience when you work with students *and* colleagues. Most teachers I have met are generous of spirit and willing to share and grow professionally with their colleagues. There will be some who "know it all," some who will not share their tips with you, and some who may even criticize your lessons unfairly. If you feel a colleague fits the latter description, unless he or she affects your ability to teach, don't let it bother you. It takes too much energy to wonder why Mr. Smith or Ms. Bell neglected to tell you that your class is waiting for you in a different room.

Do You Float?

To teachers who are called "floaters" the expression "sink or swim" takes on a new meaning. I have had to share my classroom with teachers who came in wheeling their little carts holding their books, papers, plans, and everything else they need. I would feel so sorry for them most of the time—I say most of the time because I still have not gotten over the floater who had no respect for my classroom and I always had to straighten up the room when he left. That is why I want to offer you some advice if you are unlucky enough to be the one to have to float from classroom to classroom.

First thing you should do is talk to the teacher with whom you will be sharing the room. Set up a working agreement that defines some basic ground rules you can both live with. I suggest you ask if you may have a small section of the room for yourself, with a desk and a file cabinet. (If not, you might try negotiating for a drawer.) You should also ask if you might have one bulletin board for your class to use to make them feel a part of the room and not a "visitor" in someone else's space. Most teachers will cooperate, but occasionally one will resent your presence as much as you resent having to push your curriculum around on a cart. The good news is you will not have to do this too long, because you will get seniority and the rookies will inherit your carts.

Field Trip Protocol

Toward the end of the year, many teachers become aware they are running out of steam, their students are restless, and the classroom is hot. (Unless you are lucky enough to be in an air-conditioned school.) What is a good way to alleviate this problem? Find a place that will educate your students where it is cool, where you do not have to discipline them all the time, and all of you will have a good time to boot. Well, it sounds great but to keep peace in the school, check with your coworkers to be sure they do not have exams to give or have any other conflicts on the day of the trip. I used to see red when I would be teaching half a class because half of my students were away on class trips. Posting a list of tentative field trips is a good idea to suggest. Teachers can warn you in advance that they are going to kill you for taking away too many students. Most schools have an end date when they can no longer take trips, so make sure you check the date before you make a promise you cannot keep.

HELPING SUBSTITUTE TEACHERS

What do a combat soldier and a substitute teacher have in common? If you said they both should earn hazardous duty pay, you are right!

When I went on child-care leave, I did some subbing and thought it would be fun. Often it was, but once in a while, I had to fight the urge to run out of the school ranting and raving. The students actually had the nerve to treat me just as I had treated subs when I was their age! To many students, having a substitute teacher is like having a baby-sitter, and we all know that means getting away with murder, or at least less schoolwork. So my suggestion here is to show compassion for soon-to-be-tormented subs by preparing for them. It really works to your advantage. Upon your return, you want your students to fall right back into the routines you've established.

Have a seating chart available for subs so they can see who is present right away. Have them call the attendance as well as pass around a sheet for your students to sign. I have had students yell "Present!" for every absentee and anyone cutting class. By having their signatures on a sheet of paper, you can verify who was actually in the room. Also, have your hall pass in a conspicuous place and ask the subs to make sure they inform you who left the room during class.

The most important thing to prepare is your lesson plan. After all, most of us don't know the day before that we will be ill, and you don't want to be caught without leaving a good lesson. There is no rule saying you must leave a lesson that follows what you did the day before—just have a good lesson waiting for your sub. Because I taught sex education and prejudice awareness, a substitute could not teach my lessons unless he or she was trained therein, and the likelihood of that was almost nil. But even when I taught English and

K-8, I always had a backup "generic" lesson plan. I suggest you have one, too.

It should be a lesson that your students will understand and can work with somewhat independently. I used to use self-actualization lessons. For example, I would have the students write about different kinds of conflict and relate one to their own experience. I would have handouts for them to read about different conflicts and have them figure out ways to resolve them. Substitutes can use as much or as little as they see fit.

I had one sub who, after the first part, engaged the class in a wonderful discussion and thanked me for my good lesson. I, in good conscience, could not accept the credit because he established the rapport that allowed that to happen.

Any work you have your class do in your absence should be graded by you! This way your students know you take the sub's work just as seriously as your own.

Preparing Your Students for Your Absence

If you know you are going to be absent, let your students know in no uncertain terms that you left work for them and you expect it to be done just as they would do it with you. I would also appeal to their human side and tell them that you expect them to treat a substitute teacher with utmost respect. My students were told that I had instructed any sub to give me the names of anyone who misbehaved and that there would be consequences to pay. I finally would plead with them to be nice and not embarrass me.

Evaluating Substitute Teachers

I suggest you inform your school of great substitutes and request them in your absence. Conversely, if you have a bad experience with a sub, you might ask your principal not to let him cover for you again. I still shudder at the sub who allowed my class to go wild because he couldn't control them and refused help—even when it was offered to him. Often in difficult schools, having a warm body is the only requirement needed to be hired as a substitute, and I find that a disservice to everyone involved, especially the students.

Partnerships With Local Shops, Libraries, and Bookstores

I have been invited to many bookstores as a result of this book and have learned that most of them have partnerships with schools and work hand in hand with the teachers. Many of the larger bookstores have special "Teacher Appreciation Nights" when every book in the store may be purchased by teachers at a discounted price. Some also give teachers free posters, books, and tapes. Bookstores usually have a person who is available to come to your school for storytelling. This person may also be able to help you with book sales, as a means of fundraising.

Bookstores also have storytelling times and these times should become havens for your students. Anything you can do to forge a partnership to help children love books is well worth the effort.

You might also go to local shops and ask the managers if they are willing to donate "rewards" for your students. Many stores want to help teachers and will donate small gifts that can be given to your students.

Getting Along With the "Boss"

The principal is where the buck stops. It is very important for you to have a good relationship with him. Some principals are easier to get along with than others, but my advice to you is make every effort to get into his good graces. Just as we do not like all of our students equally, neither do principals like all their staff members.

For this strategy, I went right to my friend Pearl, who is a principal, and asked her what would cause a principal to dislike a teacher's performance. She cited the following: lateness, irregular attendance, unpreparedness, idle or unruly classes, sloppy record keeping, noticeably poor student achievement, an unwarranted number of student-behavior problems, legitimate parent complaints—to name just a few.

A word of caution in your apple-polishing campaign: You want your principal to like you, but don't promise to spin straw into gold. If your principal asks you to do something you really cannot do (such as leading a chorus although you are tone-deaf), don't accept the assignment in the hope that your willingness will be appreciated so much that your poor performance will be overlooked. If the principal insists, at least you gave fair warning! On the other hand, if you want to be noticed and praised (yes, we all enjoy that!), do volunteer for tasks that you know you can do and that will serve the school while showing off your talents.

THE TEACHERS' UNION

Most of us are members of a teachers' union. Because you are paying dues, you are entitled to its services. One service is to know what you can and cannot do in the classroom as well as what can and cannot be done to you. It is important for you to understand that the union is your advocate. It is also important for you to know that the union is interested in you becoming a better teacher and is there to help you with professional development issues. Unions sponsor many wonderful inservice courses at a nominal fee, and often for free.

Speak to your union rep when you feel there is a violation of your contract or if you think your administrator is not being fair to you, or if you feel that your rights are being violated. Your representative will tell you if you have a winnable grievance. She will tell you if your issue is covered by the contract and what you will need to present your case. Please try to use every communication skill you have before you file a grievance. Sometimes just talking to the principal who has given you the worst class 45 years in a row will make her responsive to your complaint and there will be no need for a hearing. The hearing should be a last resort.

Read the entire contract. I think that many of us read only the page with the salary schedules on it.

KEEP THOSE SKILLS SHARP

Many of us have great lessons that have long been a staple in our classrooms. These lessons that have never failed to spark our students' interests. Unfortunately, repetition often becomes stale and uninspiring, and after teaching the same lessons for years, we may lack the enthusiasm needed to stimulate the minds of our students. Even if you are teaching the same subject as the years before, try to find a few brand new lessons. Trying them is stimulating to you and the reward is usually a highly motivated group. Teaching is one of those jobs that we cannot allow ourselves to get too comfortable in. I strongly suggest you take any inservice courses offered to update your skills. Many teachers resisted taking computer courses and are now left in the dust. Things change. New and exciting things replace old ways and it is a good teacher who will grasp at new ideas. The best part is how much you will learn and grow professionally in the process.

THE REALLY IMPORTANT PEOPLE

Anyone teaching for more than an hour knows the best friends you can have are the school secretary and the custodians. No matter what they do to you, smile and say "Thank you." The secretary often runs the school. She knows where everything is and what paperwork has to be done for you to get raises, benefits, and the like. She also does the payroll. Need I say more? Seriously, the secretary is someone whose help you always need. Let her know how much you appreciate her.

There will always come a time or a crisis when you will need the custodian. Perhaps you are locked out of your room, a window got shattered, your shelves collapsed, or little Louise just threw up her lunch. If you have a good relationship with the custodian, he might run instead of walk.

Security guards, aides, nurses, guidance counselors, and all support staff are part of that team that makes your school work, and everyone should be appreciated and utilized. You should know the proper procedures and chain of command to reach these people when needed.

In the event of suspected abuse, know the procedure to report whatever you think is relevant. Being remiss may bring harm to a student as well as a lawsuit to your school.

PART VIII

Parting Shots

In June, when the year is winding down and everyone is anxious for the final bell and two chalk-free months, hopefully you will be able to look back and feel rewarded by your experiences. You may have touched some young people, and you may even be the person they remember in their later years when they reminisce about that wonderful teacher who made a difference. Following are a few final thoughts I'd like to share with you before I end. And once again, thank you for being that special person that you are—a teacher.

CHAPTER TWENTY-ONE

See You Next Year!

IS TEACHING WHAT YOU REALLY WANT TO DO?

I am a firm believer that teaching is a talent. Some of us have it, and unfortunately some of us don't. We all have talents and we have to recognize where they lie. I yearn to be a rock singer, but I can't carry a tune. Conversely, many rock stars would bore a class to death. You may be brilliant, but if you are not communicating with your students, nor finding pleasure in what you are doing, perhaps you should reevaluate your career choice. If you are enjoying your job but are finding the first few years difficult, don't despair—you're getting your feet wet. However, if you are unable to control a class after four or five years and dread going in—consider being a rock singer!

KEEP IN TOUCH

Before school ends, take the addresses of your students so you can keep in touch with them over the years. I still send them Season's Greetings cards and hear from many. Hearing about their personal growth over the years, and knowing you were part of it, is what teaching is all about.

THE PORTFOLIO

Most of us do something that is so creative that we actually wish we could patent our brilliance. Since many more teachers no longer stay in one school until they retire, but often move around the country, we can do the next best thing—capture our best moments. One idea is to take photographs of the projects that have been a success for you. Have samples of your lessons, the students' work, and photos of the kids in action. Then, of course, when your principal observes you and gives you a glowing report, put it in your portfolio along with any other testimonials you might receive. When a parent writes a letter telling you that you were sent from heaven, keep it in your portfolio. Always have a few disposable cameras hidden in your closet to capture the days when your students put on winning performances that cannot be expressed in words.

Holiday "Blahs"

If you are reading this in the beginning of the school year, I want you to deposit what I am going to say in the back of your mind. I call it the "Holiday Blahs." I seem to get more and more calls to motivate teachers right after and before holidays. New teachers often become disillusioned and need something to pick them up. It seems that around Thanksgiving and the Winter Break teachers hit the "brick wall." (This goes for teachers AND students as well.) Keep in mind, this is an annual event and if you feel like you are running out of ideas, questioning yourself, and are just plain exhausted, you are not alone. Luckily we have the winter and spring breaks to reenergize us and get us back on track.

Burnout Prevention

Teaching the same grade and the same subjects year after year gets to be old hat and often leads to burnout. When I began teaching I taught all subjects to third graders. After a few years I was asked to teach sixth-grade English in middle school. I was reluctant at first, but soon I learned that it was like tackling a brand new job. After many years teaching middle school English, I was trained in sex education and once again, I experienced the fun of a new position. This led to a curriculum I developed in prejudice awareness. I look back and realize I never burned out because I changed grades and subjects, and I truly think that if I hadn't been asked to, I would have fallen into the rut that many teachers find themselves in, repeating the same curriculum year after year. Ask for another grade level or consider training in another subject area. You can bet the new experience will be challenging at first, but uplifting in the long run.

ONLY A FEW MORE MONTHS 'TIL SUMMER VACATION

I warn you right now that you are going to hear from others how easy your job is because you get summers off. To those people who would belittle our job because we have so much time off, my friend, Maureen, would say, "If you are my friend, you're happy for me—if you're not, eat your heart out!" Why react defensively to deaf ears?

I know and you know that teaching is exhausting and that the summer vacation is needed for you to merely reenergize. So have a wonderful summer, do fun things for yourself, and be proud of your accomplishments—*you earned it!*

Suggested Readings

Artman, J. (1989). *Insights.* Carthage, IL: Good Apple.

Bosch, K. (2006). *Planning classroom management* (2nd ed.). Thousand Oaks, CA: Corwin Press.

Canfield, J., & Wells, H. (1994). *100 ways to enhance self-concept in the classroom* (2nd ed.). Englewood Cliffs, NJ: Prentice Hall.

Charles, C. M. (2007). *Building classroom discipline* (9th ed.). White Plains, NY: Longman.

Chase, J., & Chase, C. (1993). *Tips from the trenches.* Lancaster, PA: Technomic.

Christopher, C. J. (1992). *Nuts and bolts.* Lancaster, PA: Technomic.

Di Giulio, R. (2006). *Positive classroom management* (3rd ed.). Thousand Oaks, CA: Corwin Press.

Faber, A., & Mazlish, E. (2001). *How to talk so kids will listen.* New York: Piccadilly Press.

Fisher, R., & Ury, W. (1991). *Getting to yes: Negotiating agreement without giving in.* New York: Penguin.

Ford, C. W. (1994). *We can all get along: 50 steps you can take to help end racism.* New York: Dell.

Ginott, H. (1998). *Teacher and child.* New York: Scribner Paper Fiction.

Golub, J. N. (1994). *Activities for an interactive classroom.* Urbana, IL: National Council of Teachers of English.

Gootman, M. (2000). *The caring teacher's guide to discipline.* Thousand Oaks, CA: Corwin Press.

Kreidler, W. J. (1995). *Creative conflict resolution: More than 200 activities for keeping peace in the classroom.* Tucson, AZ: Good Year Books.

Lickona, T. (1991). *Educating for character.* New York: Bantam.

Lighter, D. (1995). *Gentle discipline.* Deephaven, MN: Meadowbrook.

Lindberg, J., & Swick, A. (2006). *Common-sense classroom management for elementary school teachers.* Thousand Oaks, CA: Corwin Press.

Pipher, M. (2005). *Reviving Ophelia.* New York: Riverhead Trade.

Ray, P. (1990). *Resolving conflict creatively.* New York: Educators for Social Responsibility.

Stone, R. (2004). *Best teaching practices for reaching all learners.* Thousand Oaks, CA: Corwin Press.

Young, P. (2004). *You have to go to school—You're the principal!* Thousand Oaks, CA: Corwin Press.

Index

Ability grouping, 126–127
Academic records, 14
Accident documentation, 23, 136
Admitting ignorance, 103–104
Admitting mistakes, 103
Advocacy for students, 153–154
"Aim" of lessons, 32
"Am I boring?," 59–60
Answering machines, 150
Anxiety:
    first day of school, 4
    reading aloud, 51–52
    test-taking and, 84
Apologies, 101
Arguments, 69
Attendance records, 98
Attention-seeking students, 83
Aural learners, 86
Average students, calling home for, 124–125

Bad behaviors (not bad students),
    83–84
Bathroom breaks, 47–50
    bathroom coupons, 48–49
    female issues, 49–50
    sign-out book, 47
    visual codes, 48
    visual pass, 48
Bathroom conditions, 49
Behavioral conduct sheets, 65
Bell-ringing, 78
Binders, 31, 36
Birthdays, 114
Blaming the parents, 149
Body language, 83
Bonding strategies, 109–117
    bending the rules, 112
    encouraging creative excuses, 112
    extracurricular activities, 114–115
    humor and being human, 109–110

"I thought of you," 115
journals and, 112–113
Lowden's Life Lessons, 91, 116
"on your side," 109
personalizing schoolwork, 111
reading aloud, 113–114
reassuring about parent conferences, 117
recognizing special dates, 114
relating personal experiences, 110
special efforts for difficult students, 111
staying neutral, 110–111
student sharing times, 115
thanking, 117
See also Empowering students;
        Self-esteem strategies
Boring teachers, 59–60
Buddy teachers, 152–153
Bulletin boards, 128
Bullies, 52–54. See also Disruptive or
        chronically misbehaving students
Burnout avoidance, 26–27, 164–165

Cafeteria, 134
Calling home:
    *67, 150
    answering machine concerns, 150
    calling *both* parents, 144
    for average students, 124–125
    letting students make call, 55
    not calling home as disciplinary strategy,
        54–55
    when to, 66
Candy as reward, 64
Choices, 51, 55–56
Chores, 81–82
Clapping technique, 76–77
Class as collective noun, 57
Class dismissal, 34
Class wrap-ups, 32–33
Classroom dynamics, 81

Classroom order and control:
    alternatives to yelling, 75–80
    avoiding confrontation, 66–74
    avoiding empty threats, 71, 98
    bathroom breaks, 47–50
    bell-ringing, 78
    clapping technique, 76–77
    controlling noise and talking, 21–22
    dismissal, 34
    "*excuse* me," 75
    gestures, 76
    "I AM WAITING," 78
    imaginary friend, 80
    infamous "teacher" stare, 75
    initials on the board, 77
    leaving classes unattended, 134–135
    lowered voice, 76
    pencil sharpening, 37–38
    permissiveness versus, 88
    praising one, 77
    principals in the classroom, 62
    recess manipulations, 80
    turning off lights, 77
    understanding tacit approval, 52–53
    visual commands, 78
    word of the day, 80
    See also Confrontation avoidance;
        Consequences; Disruptive or
        chronically misbehaving students;
        Rules; Tardiness responses
Classroom routines, changing when
    ineffective, 25
Classroom sign-out book, 47
Classrooms:
    displaying teacher diplomas, 12
    floaters and, 155
    room decoration, 11, 117
    room organization, 11
    seating arrangements, 15–17
Clerical responsibilities, 7
Collateral, 36
Collective bargaining, 159
Communication. *See* Parent-teacher
    communication; Teacher-student
    communication
Comparing students, 73–74
Competition between teachers, 154–155
Compliments. *See* Praise and recognition
Conduct sheets, 65
Confidence grading, 122
Confidentiality:
    gossip and, 154

journals and, 25–26, 113
    never promise, 87
    reporting serious issues, 25–26, 87, 113
    student records, 14
Conflict resolution programs, 152
Confrontation avoidance, 66–74
    alternatives to yelling, 75–80
    avoiding arguments, 69
    avoiding embarrassing students,
        67–68, 82
    avoiding vague allegations, 97
    describing what is seen or not seen, 97
    distraction, 74
    don't compare students, 73–74
    don't take sides, 73
    neutrality, 110–111
    not criticizing student's character, 74
    overlooking minor infractions, 70
    phrases to avoid, 68–69
    sound-off minute, 90
    starting all over, 70
    stating rules impersonally, 97
    teacher anger or lapses, 67
    using humor, not sarcasm, 68
    See also Classroom order and control;
        Fairness; Teacher-student
        communication
Consequences, 51, 63
    behavioral conduct sheets, 65
    class as collective, 57
    don't futurize, 99–100
    fairness in determining, 63
    follow-through, 105
    forcing students to lie, 72
    "hurts me more than it hurts
        you," 105
    letting students set, 21
    no forced apologies, 101
    not being prepared, 35
    not doing homework, 44–45
    rewards, 63–64
    time-out, 73
Continuing teacher education, 159–160
Cooperative learning, 81
Counselors, 6, 25, 151–152
Creative excuses, 112
Criticizing student's character, 74
Crushes on teachers, 5
Cultural differences, 76, 88–89
Cursing, 100–101
Custodial staff, 160
Custody issues, 132

Defensive parents, 23, 147
Desk drummers, 99
Diploma display, 12
Discipline. *See* Calling home; Classroom
    order and control; Consequences; Rules
Dismissal, 34
Dispensing medication, 135
Disruptive or chronically misbehaving
    students:
    bad behaviors (not bad students), 83–84
    different standards for different kids, 84
    documenting behavior, 23
    negative attention seekers, 83
    not calling home as disciplinary strategy,
        54–55
    parental defensiveness, 23
    referring to counselor, 25
    special efforts for, 111
    throwing out of class, 132
    See also Bullies; Confrontation avoidance
Distracting restless students, 74
Diversity, 88–89, 123
"Do Now" activities, 32
Documenting and record-keeping, 23
    all accidents, 23, 136
    attendance, 98
    extreme misbehaviors, 23
    getting student and parent information,
        17–18
    homework completion, 42
Dress, 4–5

E-mail, 20, 143
Embarrassment, 67–68, 82
Emergency plan, 133
Empowering students, 51
    "am I boring?," 59–60
    calls home, 54–55
    choices and consequences, 51
    classroom as sanctuary, 52
    conference for grading, 56–57
    conflict resolution programs, 152
    determining appropriate consequences, 63
    end-of-year evaluation, 61–62
    fads, 58
    lesson plan deviations, 58
    lots of quizzes, 54–55
    offering choices, 56
    "passing" reading aloud, 51–52
    power in numbers, 54
    role reversal or role-playing, 59
    setting up winning situations, 71

suggestion box, 60
    telling on perpetrators, 53–54
    understanding tacit approval, 52–53
    See also Fairness; Feedback; Praise and
        recognition; Self-esteem strategies
Empty threats, 71, 98
End-of-class activities, 24
Etiquette, 106–107
"Excuse me" smile, 75
Excuses, 112
Extracurricular activities, 114–115

Fads, 58
Fairness, 103
    admitting ignorance, 103–104
    admitting mistakes, 103
    confronting teacher unfairness,
        153–154
    determining appropriate consequences, 63
    don't demand promises, 104
    gender issues, 94–95, 106
    homework amount, 107
    inconsistent or capricious rules, 71
    keeping promises, 104
    listening, 96
    staying neutral, 110–111
    See also Confrontation avoidance;
        Empowering students
Family stereotyping, 149–150
Family visitors, 144
Feedback:
    "am I boring?," 59–60
    class wrap-up, 32–33
    end-of-year evaluation of class,
        61–62
    informal assessment of learning, 58–59
    sound-off minute, 90
    See also Empowering students
Field trips, 155–156
Fights, 90, 132–133
Films, 33, 133
First day of school:
    ending on up note, 24
    explaining rules, 21
    fun activities, 18–19
    getting student information, 17–18
    giving teacher information, 19–20
    lesson plan for, 5–6
    teacher anxieties, 4
Floaters, 155
Forced apologies, 101
Futurizing, 99–100

Gender pronouns, 1, 94–95, 106
Gender segregation, 16–17
Gestures, 76
Ginott, H., 56
Gossiping, 154
Grading:
    behavioral conduct sheets, 65
    conference with student, 56–57
    journals and, 65
    lots of quizzes, 55–56
    minimizing competition, 128
    overgrading and building self-esteem, 122
    peer grading, 65–66
    "start with a 99%," 64–65
Greeting students, 23
Group assignments, 17, 126–127
Group dynamics, 81
Gut feelings, 136

Hall passes, 48
Health issues:
    dispensing medication, 135
    menstruating girls, 49–50
    sensory disorders and learning, 86
    student medical records, 14
    sweets as rewards, 64
    teacher's well-being, 3–4
"Holiday Blahs," 164
Homework:
    amount of, 107
    assignments on blackboard, 32, 41
    class rewards for, 43–44
    collecting, 42
    helping students with, 45
    importance of, 41
    make up, 45
    numbered assignments, 42
    oops pass, 44
    parents and, 41, 147–148
    penalties for not doing, 44–45
    teaching responsibility and
        consequences, 43
    turning in blank sheet, 42
Homework buddies, 43
Humiliation. See Embarrassment
Humor, 68, 109–110

"I" messages, 94
"I told you so," 69
Incident documentation, 23, 136. See also
    Documenting and record-keeping
Independent reading, 57–58
Inservice courses, 160

Internet concerns:
    E-mail, 20, 143
    plagiarism, 72
Introductions, 19

Journals, 25–26, 65, 112–113

Language issues:
    diverse classes and, 88–89
    limiting slang, 60–61
    not overcorrecting errors, 61
"Late bloomers," 126
Leadership versus team playing, 124
Learning, informal evaluation of, 58–59
Lesson plans:
    first day of class, 5–6
    interesting deviations from, 58
    new teachers and, 6
    overplanning, 5–6
    substitutes and, 156–157
Listening, 96
Lowden's Life Lessons, 91, 116
Lying, 72, 125

Marble jar, 64
Medical records, 14
Medication, 135
Menstruation, 49–50
Mentor teachers, 4
Multicultural issues, 88–89

Neatness, 89
Negative attention seekers, 83
Negativity, 8
New teachers, 3
    first-day anxiety, 4
    learning from other teachers, 7–8
    lesson plans of, 6
Nicen Up 101, 116
Now and later cards, 18

One-on-one conferences, 56–57,
    95–96
"Only kidding," 68
Oops pass, 44

Pairing strategies, 19
Paper, 31, 38–39
Paperwork, 7
Paraphrasing, 100
Parent blame, 149
Parent involvement, 143–144, 147–148
Parent stereotyping, 149–150

Parental criticism of teacher's methods, 148–149
Parental custody issues, 132
Parental defensiveness, 23, 147
Parental expectations, 148
Parent-teacher communication, 141
  accommodating parent schedules, 142
  assuring parents, 146–147
  calling *both* parents, 144
  early intervention, 142
  E-mail, 143
  getting parent information, 17–18
  homework, 41
  introductions, 141–142
  meeting parents soon, 141
  not calling home as disciplinary strategy, 54–55
  signoff on school/class rules, 21
  tear-strips, 143
  See also Calling home
Parent-teacher conferences, 117
  student participation, 144–145
  teacher as middleman, 145–146
Peer grading, 65–66
Pencil sharpening, 37–38
Pencils, 37
Penmanship, 89
Performance, student. *See* Student performance
Personalizing schoolwork, 111
Phone numbers, 19–20
Photo gallery, 12
Phrases to avoid, 68–69
Plagiarism, 72
Politeness, 106–107
Popular culture fads, 58
Portfolio, 163–164
Power in numbers, 54
Praise and recognition:
  acknowledging improvement, 122
  avoid overpraising, 121
  enthusiastic credit for ideas, 123
  getting kids' attention, 77
  mixing criticism with, 100
  See also Empowering students; Self-esteem strategies
Prejudice awareness, 82
Principals, 62, 158–159
Privacy, respecting, 86. *See also* Confidentiality
Professionalism:
  being early, 11
  being prepared, 11, 12–13

diploma display, 12
dress, 4–5
no tardiness, 13
using slang, 60
Promises, 87, 104
Punishments. *See* Consequences

Quizzes, 55–56

Reading aloud, 51–52, 113–114
Reading independently, 57–58
Recess, 80
Record-keeping. *See* Documenting and record-keeping
Reporting incidents, 23, 136. *See also* Documenting and record-keeping
Reporting serious student personal issues, 25–26, 87, 113
Reputation of students, 87, 154
Restroom conditions, 49. *See also* Bathroom breaks
Rewards, 63–64
  for early students, 79
  tear-strips for items to be signed, 143
Role reversal, 59
Role-playing, 59
Routines, 31
Rules, 21
  avoiding empty threats, 71, 98
  establishing early, 22
  inconsistency or capriciousness, 71
  letting students set, 21
  overlooking minor infractions, 70, 112
  parent signoff, 21
  setting limits, 29
  specificity and common sense, 72–73
  stating impersonally, 97
  total not partial limits, 96–98
  See also Classroom order and control: Consequences

Safety issues, 129
  being alone with students, 134
  breaking up fights, 132–133
  cafeteria, 134
  classroom as sanctuary, 52
  dispensing medication, 135
  face the door, 131–132
  following gut feelings, 136
  giving rides to students, 135–136
  no promises of confidentiality, 87
  prescreening videos, 133

releasing students, 132
reporting serious student disclosures,
     25–26, 87, 113
school's emergency plan, 133
setting limits, 29
touching, 131
unattended classes, 134–135
understanding tacit approval, 52–53
working late, 137
Sanctuary, 52
Sarcasm, 68
School emergency plan, 133
School supplies:
  binders, 31, 36
  paper, 31, 38–39
  teacher discounts, 36, 158
School supply lending approaches, 35–38
  collateral, 36
  "owing a favor," 35–36
  selling for charity, 38
  special pencils, 37
  strings attached, 37
  swapping, 38
  teaching responsibility and
       consequences, 35
Scrap paper, 38–39
Seating arrangements, 15–17
Secretarial staff, 160
Self-esteem strategies, 121
  acknowledging improvement, 122
  beneficial fibbing, 125
  calling home for average
       students, 124–125
  comments on schoolwork papers, 127
  enthusiastic credit for ideas, 123
  handling incorrect answers, 124
  "knew you could do it," 125
  minimizing competition, 128
  overgrading, 122
  posting students' work, 128
  praise without overpraising, 121
  put-ups not put-downs, 123
  respecting uniqueness, 123
  stronger personalities and team
       playing, 124
  tracking and, 126–127
  See also Bonding strategies; Empowering
       students
Sensory disorders, 86
Sexism, 106
"Shut up," 57, 69
Sitting with students, 22, 96

Slang, 60–61
Smiling, 75
Sound-off minute, 90
Special needs students, 45
Special relative day, 144
Spelling groups, 127
Spelling tests ("torture sheets"), 65–66
Sports pressures, 85
Start-up activities, 32
Stereotyping families, 149–150
Student appearance versus behavior, 82
Student body language, 83
Student chores, 81–82
Student complaints against teachers,
       confronting teachers about, 153–154
Student conduct sheets, 65
Student crushes, 5
Student empowerment. See
       Empowering students
Student goals and expectations, 85
Student information, 17–18
  now and later cards, 18
  reading student records, 14
  respecting privacy, 86
Student noise and talking, 21–22
  desk drummers, 99
Student performance:
  acknowledging improvement, 122
  informal evaluation for lessons, 58–59
  neatness and penmanship, 89
  quality versus quantity, 89
  studying and, 84–85
  teacher goals and expectations, 6
Student personal problems:
  acknowledging feelings, 93–94
  complaints against other teachers, 102
  don't make confidentiality promises, 87
  helping or showing understanding, 83
  journals and, 112–113
  reporting serious issues, 25–26, 87, 113
Student photos, 12
Student records, 14
Student reputation, 87, 154
Student-teacher relationships. See Teacher-
       student relationships
Studying, 84–85
Substitute teachers, 156–157
Suggestion box, 60
Summer vacation, 165
Supplies. See School supplies
Support resources. See Teacher support
Sweets as rewards, 64

Tacit approval, 52–53
Tardiness responses, 79, 98
Tardy quiz, 79
Teacher competition, 154–155
Teacher dress, 4–5
Teacher emotional lapses, 67
Teacher family and friends, 3
Teacher goals and expectations, 6, 163
Teacher health concerns, 3–4
Teacher moods, 105
    "Holiday Blahs," 164
Teacher negativity, 8
Teacher performance evaluation, 61–62
    "am I boring?," 59–60
    See also Feedback
Teacher personal information, giving to
    students, 19–20
Teacher portfolio, 163–164
Teacher rest and relaxation, 26–27, 165
"Teacher" stare, 75
Teacher support, 139
    conflict resolution programs, 152
    floaters and, 155
    other teachers, 7, 152–153
    principals and, 158–159
    secretaries and custodians, 160
    student chores and helpers, 81–82
    substitute teachers, 156–157
    teacher conferences, 152
    teachers' union, 159
    See also Counselors
Teachers' union, 159
Teacher-student communication
    alternatives to yelling, 75–80
    calling at home, 95–96
    comments on schoolwork papers, 127
    futurizing, 99–100
    greeting students, 23
    interchanging gender pronouns, 94–95
    journals and, 112–113
    keeping in touch, 163
    limiting "you shoulds," 95
    listening, 96
    one-on-one conferences, 56–57, 95–96

paraphrasing, 100
respect and sensitivity, 99
simplicity and brevity, 98–99
sitting with students, 22, 96
supportive touching, 101
using "I" and "let's," 94
    See also Empowering students; Feedback
Teacher-student relationships:
    bonding strategies, 109–117
    class solutions for classroom
        problems, 116
    conference for grading, 56–57
    friendly, not buddies, 13
    guidelines for students, 116
    not taking behavior personally, 26
    over-involvement, 113
    sitting with students, 22
    See also Bonding strategies
Teaching as career, 163
Teaching skills maintenance, 159–160
Tear-strips, 143
Telling on others, 53–54
Test anxiety, 84
Thievery, 53–54
Time-out, 73
Torture sheets, 65–66
Touching, 101, 131

Unions, 159
Uniqueness, 123

Videos, 33, 133
Violence. *See* Fights; Safety issues
Visual commands, 78
Visual learners, 86
Visual pass, 48
Volunteering, 8–9

"Warm Up" activities, 32
Word of the day, 80
Workload, 8–9
Worksheet assignments, 33

Youth culture fads, 58

CORWIN PRESS

The Corwin Press logo—a raven striding across an open book—represents the union of courage and learning. Corwin Press is committed to improving education for all learners by publishing books and other professional development resources for those serving the field of PreK–12 education. By providing practical, hands-on materials, Corwin Press continues to carry out the promise of its motto: **"Helping Educators Do Their Work Better."**